2nd Edition

Marriage Rocks!

A little bit of spice is always there!!

Dr. Jaideep Singh Chadha

PUSTAK MAHAL®
Delhi • Bangalore • Mumbai • Patna • Hyderabad • London

Publishers
Pustak Mahal®, **Delhi**

J-3/16 , Daryaganj, New Delhi-110002
☎ 23276539, 23272783, 23272784 • *Fax:* 011-23260518
E-mail: info@pustakmahal.com • *Website:* www.pustakmahal.com

London Office
51, Severn Crescents, Slough, Berkshire, SL 38 UU, England
E-mail: pustakmahaluk@pustakmahal.com

Sales Centre
10-B, Netaji Subhash Marg, Daryaganj, New Delhi-110002
☎ 23268292, 23268293, 23279900 • *Fax:* 011-23280567
E-mail: rapidexdelhi@indiatimes.com

Branch Offices
Bangalore: ☎ 22234025
E-mail: pmblr@sancharnet.in • pustak@sancharnet.in
Mumbai: ☎ 22010941
E-mail: rapidex@bom5.vsnl.net.in
Patna: ☎ 3294193 • *Telefax:* 0612-2302719
E-mail: rapidexptn@rediffmail.com
Hyderabad: *Telefax:* 040-24737290
E-mail: pustakmahalhyd@yahoo.co.in

Edition : 2008

ISBN 978-81-223-0986-7

Printed at : Param Offsetters, Okhla, New Delhi-110020

This book is dedicated to
The newly weds AMAN and CHANDNI,
The veterans, KARAN and GUNEET,
THOSE WHO INTEND TO MARRY
AND
THOSE WHO INTEND TO STAY MARRIED

This is also a tribute to all those who have
SUFFERED GRIEVOUSLY, BUT ARE STILL
MARRIED !!
(valid for the original spouse only!)

Acknowledgements

I am deeply indebted to all those lovely people, none of whom, I can assure you, were idle, for sparing their valuable time to give me their views on a subject as important as marriage, especially because of its dwindling importance in the minds of our youth and the fickleness of the ones who are married.

Special thanks to Mr. Sam Panwar and Mrs. Anita Bansal for their patience while reviewing the manuscript.

A great big thank you to Mr. Bharpur Singh for the cartoons that he created. You are the judges of his talent.

Last, but not the least, to my publishers, Pustak Mahal, Delhi, and Mr. Rohit Gupta, for his confidence in me.

Contents

Preface

After the hugely successful Please Mom! It's My Life! which is based on understanding 'self' and how to manoeuvre through the highways of life, I thought of writing about the most important aspect of our second coming, that is – when we travel on the marriage highway.

By this time, we are expected to be mature enough to avoid the many pitfalls on this journey. The problem here is that there are no coaches or traffic policemen to guide us through and show us the way to a happy and fulfilled married life. Parents are always there to guide us to the best of their capabilities, but their guidance is never enough. We can hardly call ourselves 'matured' or say that we have understood everything that we needed to understand, even after the gruelling first half; we arrive battered and bruised, at the starting line of the second half of our lives. All of a sudden we are loaded with an added responsibility of a partner, whom we do not know, at least in the Indian scenario, a person who has his or her own fears, idiosyncrasies, his or her own expectations from life and from the relationship.

The most difficult thing in human existence is to be able to understand 'the self'. We go through life trying to do just that because this is the basis of all our relationships. We first have to understand the terms "What am I?" or "Who am I?" or "Why am I here?" or "What do I exactly want?" and "From whom"; "What can I offer in return for what I get?" and "What do I have to do?" Suddenly, we realise that 'self' has been taken over by 'ego'.

From then on, our ego guides our relationships. Here I might add that ego-guided relationships are a one-way ticket to disaster.

Human relationships you know, are a pain, and extremely difficult to maintain; but none of them needs as much nurturing, care, love, understanding, patience, trust, dedication, forgiveness, and finally divine intervention, as the husband and wife relationship.

The scenario thus far is grim. Here is a person who is grappling with himself, trying to settle down in life, trying to make a success out of whatever he has been educated in and he has hardly any money with which to fight it out. Suddenly, he is expected to marry and settle down and try to make the most of what he possesses. He has not learnt the basics yet, no matter how much he may want the world to think otherwise; how does he learn to understand the other person, since he is still trying to make himself understood!

If it involved only the husband and wife, I am sure after initial hiccoughs, they would succeed. But there are other forces involved which only serve to make the situation more complicated. The well-known 'in-laws' syndrome, parents on both sides and coming of children who create their own situations at every stage of their lives. This is a circus.

If the two characters in this play finally progress to the third stage, which is the marriage of their children, they are applauded for a job done well and that all their responsibilities are now over. Little do they know that their responsibilities will never be over. On the contrary, they will be magnified.

There are, but only a few who pass through this journey, without tripping or getting their clothes snagged in the roadside barbed wire. They will pass through other pitfalls relatively easily, but putting up with each other proves to be the sternest test of all. In earlier days, they stayed together, no matter what. These days, with ladies being advanced in education, matters relating to self-sufficiency and heightened egos, temptations to give in midway and travel on their own have increased manifolds. ***'Obviously, treading the lonely furrow is not without its share of dangers'.***

This book is like a wake-up call for those who are in the second phase of their lives. In fact, the reason for writing this book was to make people aware that without the institution of marriage, matters will go out of hand, where morality will be the greatest sufferer. To belong to someone is a matter of great relief and happiness. This aspect is most obvious in people who have no one to call their own. People who have lost their parents, siblings and their spouses, people who do not have children in their marriage... such people have such a large void in their lives that a whole planet can easily get lost in it. It is only when we have people in our lives and do not care about them and are prepared to let them go so easily that repentance comes sooner than later.

Relationships exist only because we are in them. We make them important. It is just like gold. It is valued only because of us and because it is so scarce. Animals have no value for it. If there was perpetual darkness, would we able to differentiate gold from lead, copper or even iron? It is said that if sand was as scarce as gold, we would have kept sand in a vault and society would have given it the same stature as gold.

So, if the institution of marriage is so important to most of us, then why is that we give it the least importance. We should realise here that once we get into a relationship, we have to completely surrender ourselves to it and only then can we banish our ego.

Here is wishing you all a happy, prosperous and lasting… wedded life!

PART 1

The Birth of an Institution

Never have so many people roamed the streets with their heads in their hands, pulling out hair by the handful; never have so many men become bald without having to pull out even a single strand of hair, just because they can't get the answer to one simple question... why? Oh Blessed, why?

I am one of those who are married and constantly wonder why. My mind has reverberated with the word WHY so many times in the last 32 years that there is a constant hum in my head. Sometimes that hum becomes a humming bird's song and sometimes it becomes thunder, accompanied by lightning and all kinds of scary sounds. When I am really scared or angry, I look towards the skies and wonder where those so called philosophers were, who initiated this institution called marriage.

I want to do terrible things to them. But before one does something terrible to anyone, one must always delve into the whys of it. Why did they want to do something like this? Knowing the unfathomable mindset of the human species, knowing fully well that God created the two sexes only for a specific purpose, where compatibility for a few minutes was no problem; no one could foresee the disastrous effects a prolonged union would produce. Despite being armed with grave knowledge, they still went ahead and created something so complicated that no one has ever been able to understand till date. It has been centuries already. I wonder if they are repenting their actions, sitting cosily, up there in the clouds. Or do they have a naughty smile on their lips, enjoying each moment of what they are witnessing?

This 'why' has two parts — why did humans want to create such an institution; and why did another set of humans agree, and like a flock of sheep, dive into it, head first? Let's analyse it and see where they went wrong. Or right!

Remember the Stone Age? Some people say that man had just stepped out of the shoes of an ape at that point of time. First things first, I don't agree with what the anthropologists say. That we owe our existence to apes! That apes walked on all fours initially, and then one fine day, started walking on their twos. Suddenly that made such a huge difference that the final product, man, instantaneously became intelligent and all that. So why didn't all the apes, gorillas, orang-utans, langoors and monkeys decide to walk on their twos and become humans too? Why are they what they are, and we what we became? I am sure any gorilla would want to get a changeover, if it was shown a photograph of Sophia Loren or Cary Grant, depending upon its sex and preferences. The question is why didn't they, when change was in vogue? When they had the chance? There are so many apes still moving around. Why are they here? Don't they know that they are supposed to evolve into a creature called man?

The answer is simple. Because, we are not the by-products of apes. We are the originals; we did not evolve from the monkeys, though we do behave like them most of the time.

We are humans. And don't even think about Eve being created from the rib of Adam. Why from the ribs of Adam? Why couldn't Adam be created from the ribs of Eve? Just because we are a male-dominated society, our thinking is also male-warped. Eve could have been created just as Adam was. Just for argument sake, even if she was created from Adam's rib, which one was it? The second, the floating twelfth, or was it the extra cervical rib?

What I don't understand is, why make things more complicated than they are already? Why can't we be happy and accept the fact that we could have been created in the same way as other beings were created? I mean like the giraffes and the lions, the birds and the bees? They say only two humans were created — one was Adam, the male and the other was Eve, the female. I wonder who named them Adam and Eve. Since they were primitive and did not possess a recognised language, how did they ever manage to give each other such romantic names like Adam and Eve? They also had the sense to realise that the male had to have a masculine name and the female should have a feminine name.

And why bring Adam and Eve into it? Just imagine for a moment that Adam and Eve were the first two human beings, created in the image of God. Then they had two sons — Cain and Abel. Then, one day Cain decided to kill Abel. I wonder, why? They say he was jealous. I wonder, of whom? There were only four of them and still they could not get along. ***Then, how can anyone expect us to get along when there are millions and trillions of us now!*** So that left Adam, Eve and Cain. So where did the others come from? Are we the products of incest? There had to be more of our kind in the world of the Stone Age, people who produced other people. But no! We have to glamorise everything because of the storyteller who resides in us. We love stories.

Okay, let's say that we were there for just the same reason as other creatures were. The difference was that the others discovered that one was different from the other anatomically, and instinct told them that they were supposed to procreate as per those differences. Or, they just copulated and the progeny arrived to their utter surprise. And then, there were those who laid eggs, and others of their kind happily came out of those eggs. Some discovered more pleasurable modes of procreation, just as humans did. But then, why did humans have to make each other into an art form just because of their anatomical and procreative differences?

I believe women did not exactly look like Cleopatra in that era, and men did not have that Adonis feel. They looked more like their nearest relatives. Even then, the attraction to the opposite sex was as prevalent as it is today. And they did not even have designer clothes, if you please. Initially, it was the fig leaf, we are told, which gave way to some clothes made out of animal furs that barely covered them. If the attraction between the two sexes was possible even then, I mean with the looks that those ancestors had, devoid of the designer clothes and other products of enhancement considered so essential today, then we can safely say that even if we had looked like our facial x-rays, then too the attraction to the opposite sex would have been there.

So, move over, ye beauty queens, looks have nothing to do with it. And stop wasting money on clothes and perfumes that everyone seems to be spending fortunes on. It has been confirmed that in the final analysis, it is a simple matter of some chemicals that all living beings secrete in various parts of their brains. Perfumes might even mask that chemical. We now know that the prairie rats secrete some special chemicals, which can even block the pregnancy of the female rat if it had been impregnated by a rat which was not in the good books of the first party. Or if it is felt that rights had been usurped by the second party! I would call it 'the jealousy chemical'.

Women always go for the testosterone look, the 'square jaw' look as they call it. The odd thing is that the women in question did not even know why they went for this particular look. For men in that era had no shaving kits and those were certainly early days for barbers to set up shop. So women could not have gone for the testosterone look with the beard covering the supposedly 'square jaw'.

But humans of the Stone Age were sure one hell of a lucky breed. They did not have a language, they had no religion, they had no country and they had no homes that they called their own. These are all the things that are considered so essential today that people have killed each other because of them and continue to do so. Most of all, they had no woman or man whom they called their own or who belonged to them or they to them. Any man could carry off any woman as a one night stand and no one minded it, one single bit. Strange, isn't it, considering today's scenario? Today, if someone does any such thing, society frowns and the wife kills. And so would the husband. What a waste! God! If I have had a past life in the Stone Age, wouldn't I love to know the details of what all I did and to how many.

Most importantly, they did not have to earn a living. They did not have an office to go to. They had no nagging bosses and no wives or children that they cared to call their own. They had no bills to pay. They did not have to stay awake through the night to see a one-day cricket match only to find out painfully that it was all a waste of time for Indian cricketers had rigged it. The only problem arose when a predator decided to make a meal out of them. Even then, most of them survived.

A bachelor is a person who doesn't have to leave the party that he has just begun to enjoy.

It makes me feel very comfortable to note that men were as foolish then as they are now. Imagine, with everything going well with all these goodies thrown in, this young fool comes from nowhere to spoil the party. He decides to get ownership rights. He wants one particular woman all to himself because his legs turn to jelly the moment he sees her. The word LOVE had not been coined though.

This new development must have been vehemently objected to in technicality… at least initially, by the other members of the clan. Later, they too succumbed to the disease and did the same thing. But I am sure things must have become complicated, because as night fell, and testosterone and oxytocin levels went up, people must have gone into a tizzy. This woman belongs to X, that one belongs to Y. In the ensuing confusion, I am sure there would have been some miscalculations too. Peace must have been shattered, because till the recent developments, women were considered a community commodity. All because they were supposed to be the weaker sex! Of course all that changed in the Amazonian era, where women were the more powerful of the two sexes.

Now we know that women were not so backward after all. Recently in Germany, they have found dildos and other sex gadgets in the newly discovered Stone Age caves. That only means that women had a mind of their own even then. They must have discarded men as and when they felt like or did not feel like it. This is the most important discovery because it just opens up a whole new Pandora's Box about sex habits of the so-called 'just graduated apes'.

It is said that necessity is the mother of invention. I just wonder about the women of the Stone Age. What was the necessity of those gadgets when they had at their disposal, all those hulks to choose from?

Ah yes! I was on the subject of this fool. He must have fallen for her like a ton of bricks or some thing of similar weight, since no one had developed bricks back then. How he must have suddenly hated the idea of his woman being carried off by his clansman and decided to fight for her! The peaceful atmosphere must have been shattered by violence. In fact, before this, there was never any reason for these people to be violent. I ask you, what would they be violent over? Food was never that big a problem, because they ate everything, plants and animals and some of them did not mind eating each other and drinking the soup. They had no problem over building up of homes or condominiums or property rights or rates, they never had fancy modes of conveyance which they had to register and keep locked lest some wayward person might steal them. They did not have to stay perpetually tense so that they could rise up the corporate ladder. Prostitution was not a profession, yet. Pornography was not an issue because no one wore clothes. Basically they had no issue in life which caused them heartburn.

It was not till the woman factor came in. This young romantic fool, who decided to have propriety rights over

her, forgot what a good thing they had already going for them. They had total access to variety! This beats all logic. Why would he have wanted to do away with that? Must have been stark crazy… raving mad! They had not even developed that drink that that made men mad, which was later called 'alcohol' by society. As I said, this act must have been objected to by others of the male species. Also, I am sure, by members of the female species, because another emotion had been incorporated into the virgin minds, thanks to Cain. This was jealousy. And as you know, jealousy has a very rabid rate of spreading. Soon, other young studs must have realised that they too have this funny attraction towards a particular woman. Fights over females would have become rampant.

Anyway, things would still have been manageable. Everything would have gone on well until two studs fell for the same woman or two women fell for the same man. Things must have become very messy then.

By then the older ones who had already fired their last salvos and lost interest in these mundane issues, must have sown the seeds of 'society' where by all people had to stick to rules laid down by them. These oldies were the precursors of modern day philosophers. ***Naturally, all philosophers had to be old because young people concentrate on stuff below the waist, whereas for old men, it is all a waste.*** These are the people I want to do terrible things to. They were the ones who decided that man must not fight over a woman. If he was interested in one and if the woman also showed some degree of interest in the male, they were to get entangled into a web of their own creation. They dubbed it marriage, and touted it as an institution.

To make things interesting, these so-called philosophers must also have thrown in a few rules like loyalty to one's

partner, flirtation was something to be frowned upon, adultery was a big no-no and so on. In addition, they must have added some rules of the fledgling concept of religion, thus creating relationships, like father, mother, brother, sister, aunt, the in-laws, etc. Now, it became a big extended happy family. Or, it was supposed to be so.

Then the inevitable happened. The married male of the species got bored with the love of his life and naturally started looking around. His eyes rediscovered all that was available to him all along. His attention settled on the ones who had not yet been asked for or the ones who had other ideas. It was not his fault at all. The chemicals in his brain were being developed because of which the married man's hitherto tunnel vision, which had looked mostly at his own woman, developed peripheral vision into which other women fell, almost like bolts from the blue. And, he loved it.

Currency in some form would have developed by now. So a new breed of women realised that there was profit to be had in this concept called marriage of which they ought to be a part of. Hence the modern day creed of 'women of the world' was born. She has been given many names in all societies and since we are not in the name calling business, we shall not put a name to them.

It was not only men who developed all encompassing peripheral vision. Married women developed the same. They too discovered hulks hovering along the path.

Men also realised that the fruit in the other man's plate is tastier than the one in your own after their roving eyes settled on married women. And thus extra-marital affairs began... followed by fights and disagreements between men and women in the institution. The good old philosophers noted these developments and since by then society had begun to protect itself by an arrangement called Law; they took these warring couples to the law agencies which decided what to do with them. It was mostly decided that these people could break the vows that they had taken when they got married and that they could live separately after the man paid a penalty in the form of alimony, which in other words meant that he had to suffer for the rest of his life. It was also a deterrent for other fools not to dive into this institution without knowing the pitfalls well. But then, man has a very short memory and he went on doing whatever he should not be doing. This holds true of the women as well.

Women are considered to be the weaker of the two sexes and her survival in a male-dominated world depended upon the protection provided by the institution of marriage. So she was naturally very keen to get married for the social status that marriage offered, and also the financial and physical security that was a built-in offer. In case the marriage did not last, then she was not the loser in any case. That is how she began to revere the term 'ALIMONY', which men hated.

The philosophers also put in a clause that society would recognise only those children as legal who were born in matrimony. Suddenly, men and women all over began to crave for children, and since the heritage factor had been established, they wanted to produce children so that their name would be carried forward. There was a riot of sorts, heading straight to the wedding altar. Anyone who succeeded in getting married, man or woman, began to think that their journey had already been blessed with a happy ending. This is how Hollywood and Bollywood made their movies and continue to do so. After the two get married, there is a caption which automatically arrives on the screen, announcing THE END, FINISH, and AND THEY LIVED HAPPILY EVER AFTER!

Little did they know that the fight had just begun!

And thus began the eternal love-hate relationship between man and woman.

There were some intelligent men who did not want to get married. Their physical needs were provided by the members of the same sex. These people were then recognised as gay, in modern day parlance. Alexander the Great was one such intelligent man. He had a few wives to provide a family and was in love with a man! No wonder he conquered almost the entire world!

But the fact remained that people still were hugely interested in marriage and went on getting involved with that aspect of their lives. After hundreds of years, they continue to get married, some happily and others live unhappily together, and still others decide to part company, legally. It came to be known as 'divorce'.

A doctor friend, fresh from his visit to Sweden was dumbstruck, on the verge of being shell shocked.

"Doc!" he said, "People in Sweden don't marry anymore. About 80%-90% of them are having live-in relationships. Some of them have children, some don't. They have banned prostitution. Just an exercise in futility! Who needs prostitutes when women are available all the time and for free? But that is the country which has pioneered pornography and made into an art form, a hobby, something which need not be looked down upon. They shoot these films in open parks where one would be picnicking with his family, small children might be enjoying a game of Frisbee, a young mother would be pushing a pram with her baby in it; and just 20 yards away, a pornographic movie is being shot in full view. The action would evoke just a cursory glance from the general public. They just accept these things. In India, there is a riot even if some people are caught kissing. But then, that is Sweden! We don't care what they do. We have our own double standards of morality to worry about."

The reason the Swedes stopped caring about matrimonial issues is another WHY and can easily be a subject of research. Alimony might just turn out to be the largest obstacle.

We have come a full circle. Humans were naked, started with the fig leaf, went on to wear clothes barely enough to cover them to being over-dressed. Now we have reached a stage where they wear clothes which barely cover them and would rather be naked. They have reached the orgy state and wife swapping. They would rather not have a wife. Fifty years from now, people would probably have no reason to ogle at nude photographs or pornographic movies because all that the younger generation is going to wear is the fig leaf. Maybe, not even that! What the pornographic movies show would be seen everywhere. Prostitution might not exist because women and men will be easily available, for the institution of marriage would have been phased out.

I am neither here nor there. The institution of marriage is still here. I will undergo the same changes that my ancestors went through.

PART 2

The Chemistry

By all means marry. If you get a good wife, you will be happy. But if you get a bad one, you will become a philosopher.

...so said Socrates

Till now, we have solved the basic question. Why did man and woman become what they finally became? The questions that still linger on are many and we will take them up as we go along.

The first one has to be:

If they could not live without getting married, then why not live peacefully?

The other day I saw the x-ray plate of a very beautiful woman. I compared it with the x-ray plate of a very ugly man. Both were equally ugly and may I add, equally scary.

So, when God put unequal amounts of soft tissues on the skulls, and other parts of men and women, they began to look different and needless to say, women definitely had a better score. Not all though! That was probably why men put women on pedestals, making them into the art form that they are considered today, all the while forgetting the x-ray look.

But women were equally attracted to the males of the species. It was the chemistry between men and women that was responsible for the whole thing. If they had let it be till that point, nothing would have mattered. But their attraction usually ended in the institution called marriage. The basic attraction was all because of hormones secreted by various parts of the brain, phenylethylamines, or PEA, the oxytocins, the pheromones, the testosterones and the oestrogens. Humans, males or females, are totally flabbergasted at the way they behave, the moment they see their counterparts. These emotional sensors are not even in the brain. They are in the nose, say the scientists.

There was a school of thought promulgated by Aristophanes in the play by Plato *Symposium*, which suggests that in the beginning, there was only one body which housed both the male and the female. This arrangement gave great satisfaction to the humans because of their self-sufficiency. In their over-zealousness, they planned to attack the Gods themselves. Zeus punished them by creating separate bodies for the males and females. This caused intense pangs of separation in the humans. Zeus, then, relented and introduced the activity called 'intercourse', something which has made men and women busy.

There is no need to be confused. You have help at hand. A master, if I bestow this title upon myself, has presented himself at your doorstep. I intend to solve all mysteries that have ever crossed your mind on this issue.

Ever since Romeo and Juliet looked at each other and fell like a ton of bricks, producing tremors in Mangolia, behaviour has changed. So has the attire! Dress designers could not have had it better since the 'Planet of the Apes' hit theatres. In fact, things changed in almost all aspects of the game. Be it in the field of lavishing presents on each other, or going to eating joints, or flaunting their transport or modes of entertainment. Society also gained much because the lovers had to be dressed in the best, culinary habits had to be the best and the best in the rest… whatever that may be. In those days, stationery used for expression of their innermost emotions had to be the best. These days, stationery is no longer in vogue. SMS and e-mails have taken over. But in olden days, people in the business of producing these articles for the art of expression of love, had to be one jump ahead of the lovers.

Women marry because they think that their husbands will change one day. Men marry because they think that their wives will never change.... Both are mistaken.

And people all over the world continued to get married.

The rules were the same for the ones who were involved in a situation where the marriage was arranged. The couple could marry only after reaching a particular age. Despite those age restrictions, cultures of the world differed. Indians were definitely different. They had child marriages and made the two pine for each other till they were of a certain age. I am sure some of them were attracted to others of the species during this waiting period followed by chaos. Then there were people in India who decided that the woman was married to one man but available to the rest of the clan. The woman would never know who her real husband was. I believe such customs do exist even now. Anyway, we were talking about the age at which these youngsters were admitted into the institution of marriage.

The philosophers decided that humans should be matured by the time they reach 18 years of age. Hence it was decreed that 18 would be the age at which boys and girls would be eligible to marry. Suddenly there was a riot of parents running to get their children married when they turned 18. This magic figure of 18 was later chosen as the age when they could have a driving license, have sex and vote. Children could not wait for 18 to arrive!

"You know what I did before I married??... anything I wanted to."

...Henry Youngman

Here comes the question you knew was coming.... What made you make that decision to marry?

I put this question to many people, both young and old. You know what the majority of them came up with. Such profound wisdom about the most important turning point of their lives!

They said, "I really don't know!"

I told them that 'I don't know' was not a valid answer. They came up with the following excuses:

- It is the done thing, no?
- My parents wanted me to marry.
- I wanted stability and companionship; a husband to look after you.
- I wanted children and a family; a wife (or a husband) to look after you when you grow old.
- Society does not accept single people.
- If you do not marry, what else can you do?
- If we do not marry; sexual frustration would creep into our lives. We will keep looking for sex everywhere. Our minds will be so preoccupied with it that our productivity in our work will suffer.

I looked at my own reason for getting married. I was barely 23. One look and I was hooked. But when I volunteered for the 'dekho', I had already decided that I needed to get married early. I have never analysed the why of the need to get married at all; but now that I am writing this book, I am forced to look back. For me, I think being married was a forgone conclusion. I think my reason was to have a person who would be mine and I would belong to her. That sense of belonging was very important to me. Your parents are not just your parents; they are also the parents of your siblings. Your siblings are not just your siblings; they have other siblings too. So I wanted someone who would be just mine.

Now the question was when. That was decided by the fact that my family medical history was so ominous that the chances of my not being around for too long were fairly bright. Most men of my family died around 50 due to one reason or the other but mostly because of heart attacks. My own father died at the age of 45 because of leukaemia. That was the clincher. I had to get my first born settled before I copped it.

And, you? Let me make a guess. In your case, you saw, you fell, she kicked you in the head and you said, "I do!"

I agree it happens that way sometimes. But mostly, the hormones work up and the mind starts working with a single-minded dedication… to 'get' the girl. The girl does not have to be the girl of your dreams. She has to be a girl. Period. Sheer peer effect! Your friend is going out with a girl and you don't have one, and you have to equalise the score. Without realising the pitfalls, you want to go out with one. It is to 'get' the girl; marriage is nowhere in the agenda.

In olden days, quite a few boys and girls waited for their parents to get them hitched to a suitable partner. Not that the hormones were not working then. They were, but not overtime. They were still controllable. In our times, girls and boys did not even shake hands when introduced. They just said 'hello'. Hence physical intimacy was a little slow in developing. These days, they shake hands. The physical thing has already come in as step one. So the step two becomes much easier. Step three and four are just a stone throw away. Not so easy though! One has to work hard at it.

Let me guess some more. To court the woman, you had to be at your best all the time, which obviously you were. Your language had to be impeccable. Your purse perpetually loaded with money, your own or borrowed. Your visual field was totally devoid of peripheral vision. It was more like that of a donkey with blinkers. The world thought you were pathetic, but you had other ideas. How do I know all this? I went through all the procedures with flying colours. I was a pro. In fact, sometimes I thought that it was I who invented the art of wooing a woman. Right? Wrong! This had already been invented by Romeo and his peers ages ago.

Rodney Dangerfield had written the all-important words, which fell on my retinal blind spots. I say spots because other normal and intelligent people have one blind spot. I had a dozen or more, of them. So no matter where the image fell, there was a blind spot waiting to gobble it up. Imagine, if only darkness did not arrive only at night, but was there throughout the day always. Then we would not have been able to differentiate between gold and lead, young and old, man and woman, Mercedes Benz cars and a bike, and the rich and poor. The moment it becomes daylight, we can suddenly see the differences between all these things. Suddenly we can see women, and women can see gold, and men begin to see Mercedes Benz cars, and all our troubles begin.

Rodney dangerfield wrote: "My wife and I were happy for twenty years. Then we met!"

I told you that I could never understand what this gentleman intended to communicate through these words of wisdom. It was much later that I realised, that I was supposed to do was to rotate my antennae and think why he was saying that. Had I cared to rotate my antennae, I would have got the answer 33 years back. But who had the time or the inclination in those happy blissful hours of day dreaming?

These words were from a modern sage! He had seen it all. But then I had to learn from my own blunders. As, of course you, too. If we had stayed away from this species, every thing would have been fine. But the romantic stars, shining ever so brightly in our eyes give us a very different picture.

Okay…. Your next step had to be progress towards the field of wedded bliss. You missed the advertisement in the newspaper too, didn't you? This was put in by a guy who had failed in the mission 'get the girl'.

The advertisement said "wanted a wife"
The next day he received over hundred
letters urging him to "take mine!"

For you, no soap was good enough, no perfume fragrant enough and no clothes decent enough to be worn for dates. Oh, the pain of depravity! Why was God so unkind to give you the unkindest cut of all? Such a total lack of the basics of romance! How you wanted to be sucked into the quagmire of love! I know all that she must have said to make you feel like Sir Lancelot coming victorious from the battlefield. You felt like a superman, and without even knowing it, you became the sacrificial lamb. You don't agree? You will! Seriously speaking, you should have known about the advertisement.

On second thoughts, how would you have known about the married responses? You, in the final analysis are not to be faulted on that one. This malady had to come in as a part of your destiny. It was written. You had to go through it for there was no way around it. But, you have to admit it. It was all your doing from the very beginning. For you wanted the girl, didn't you?

They say that, "Women inspire men to great things and then prevent them from achieving them."

So right!

Finally, the day came when your dreams came true and you thought you had finally made it. Made it? To what? The excitement of the big day is bound to be over. In our days, that feeling lasted longer because the physical aspect of the union was still to be consummated. That was the main course in the celebrations. Most people in the olden times dreamt of things to come. There was anticipation and when it did finally come, the effect on the married couple lasted for a long long time. But these days, everything is already done and dispensed with before the D-Day. The young ones have to be sure if they are physically, mentally and emotionally compatible. Nevertheless, the newness of the relationship keeps it alive for some more time, till the two partners start going to their respective workplaces. Didn't you know that everyone works these days? So, let me tell you what happens next.

Your future depends upon your dreams.
So don't waste time: Go to bed.

But you are already up and kicking. Who gets leave from the office for honeymooning these days? You leave for your office at 8:30 in the morning and so does your newfound wife. If you have separate modes of conveyance, which is convenient, then all you can do is to talk to each other on that wonderful invention called the cell phone. Initially, you make the effort of meeting your wife for lunch, but as the month ending targets and other levels to achieve arrive, you begin to think that the effort is just too much. You end up eating lunch on the seat of some motor cycle parked in a corridor of the office complex or sitting in the cramped place you call your rest room in the office. The days seem never-ending.

You turn around and see the multitude of tired-looking young men and women doing the same. You begin to wonder if this was all that you had hoped for. Before getting married, there were visions of a loving, doting woman, welcoming you with piping hot lunch, and when you came home in the evening, she would be there, looking radiantly lovely. Your bath was ready; the bottle of beer in the freezer, with the shredded chicken you love so much as a starter… exactly like your mother did for your father. Nothing of that kind happened. Coming home for lunch was impossible. When you come home in the evening, you find the woman you married in the kitchen, with an apron on, hair dishevelled, going hither and thither. She barely has time to say 'hello' because a hungry household eagerly waits dinner. After she has cleaned up, she is too pooped up to respond to any overtures that you might have had in mind, that is if you had any energy left yourself. Well, no point crying bucketfuls of tears here. It was all your fault to begin with.

You had always wanted a wife who was career oriented. She was expected to earn a pile and so would you. At the end of the first year, the two of you are wondering aloud "WHAT HAPPENED!", if you last that long, that is! You have it all. You have a lovely educated wife, who is working shoulder to shoulder with you, earning her bit as you always wanted; but then why are you not happy and satiated? The lady wanted a smart and handsome man in the I.T. industry. She has him. He earns tons of money. You don't want children. He has the same thoughts. You have already started paying up the instalments for the flat, you have a car, and everything else you wanted, except the energy to enjoy what is yours.

So why are you not happy?
Why do you feel like committing suicide?
Why are you sad?
Why are you wanting your bachelor days back?

Because, folks, you never took marriage with any serious conviction. You took it as an experiment. For you, it was just fun and games. You wanted to have your cake and eat it too. There was no commitment. Did you ever look at your mother seriously? She just fell on your retinal blind spot. So you did not notice how she slaved and worked throughout her married life. In her days, there was commitment to the cause. She dedicated her life to her husband and children. Are you ready to do it? Are you ready? To give up your ideals of being a career woman?

And you, sir? What are you ready to give up? Those dreams of becoming a Tata or Birla at the age of 25, own half of the country, drive a flashy car and possess the latest brands. You will have to give up all that and start going slow. Inhale the fragrance of marriage. Know the person you got married to. Have total commitment towards your partner. Think of building a home first. The house can come later.

Some mothers-in-law are like clouds. The moment they disappear, the day suddenly gets brighter.

The wife no longer wants to stay in the house listening to the mother-in-law telling her stories she is not interested

in, or to end up cooking food for the entire household and the neighbourhood, if her mother-in-law could have her way! She is against the concept of keeping a servant. After all, when she got married a thousand years ago, she had to do all the work herself. That too after she had six children! She did not complain. So why does her daughter-in-law have to be so soft, a sissy. If she has to go out to work, no one is stopping her. But she cannot run away from her duties at home.

Can't her *bahu* make breakfast for the family after giving them bed tea? She loves bed tea, ***in bed***. After all, that is why the Brits called it 'bed tea' to begin with. And then she can make lunch for the people at home and pack tiffin for her husband and herself. There is nothing to it really. All it needs is good time management. What seems to be the problem here? Everything can be done side-by-side. While the bed tea is being made, she can cut the vegetables and wash the *dal*. While the vegetables are being cooked, the *dal* will be hooting away in the pressure cooker. By the time the dough is ready for the chapattis, the *dal* is ready. The rice should be soaked the night before. While the chapattis are being made, the rice is all set. So, if you really manage your time well, there is nothing to it really. These days, the casseroles are so handy. They keep the food hot and piping.

(Hey, mother-in-law! In your days, you didn't have to go to work in schools or I.T. or call centres. For good time management, these good ladies have to cater to the time wasted in queues for buses, coming and going. You were always at home and had only your household work to look after!)

But the daughter-in-law has to go out to work. Once out of the house, she heaves a sigh of relief which joins other sighs of relief coming from other young ones leaving for their offices. If she has conveyance of her own, things are easier. Otherwise, she joins the multitude of workers in the never-ending lines for buses and trains.

They join others of their kind in thousands of workplaces, exchange gossip and work, their eyes on targets they have to achieve. After work is over, she joins thousands in queues for the return journey. What they dread is coming back home to hungry people with mouths wide open, waiting for the daughter-in-law to come and make dinner or whatever goodies that she can conjure.

Since the mother-in-law does not like the idea of servants, housekeeping has to be done, which includes washing of utensils and clothes. Thank God for the machines which are of help, otherwise the dear *bahu* would have a tougher time. If her husband agrees to the servant, the mother-in-law makes sure that the servant leaves before he or she can find his or her feet in the household. The *saas* can barely tolerate the typical smell these people produce. No way will she let the servant touch and wash her utensils, her clothes or handle crockery, and other things in her home. And, who can trust servants, in any case? They can kill everyone at home and take away all that you have collected over the years. Also, when one gets used to them, they decide to leave for a few more rupees. After all, what is their relationship to you anyway… a few rupees? So why become dependent on them? The best thing is to stay away from the quagmire of convenience and be self-sufficient, like she was.

So what happens next? Two tired bodies and minds searching for reserves! Your wife who was so perky and full of life before, is now haggard and tired, putting on a brave front. In the early days of married life, you are keen to take the love of your life to a party or two, or to a movie or a restaurant. Correct? You bet! So, when you come back, totally pooped, do you think sex is such a good idea? That act which brought such wonderful fantasies and pleasure in the pre-marriage days is now a tedious chore! Have you started feeling that way already? If you have, baby, you are in trouble.

That just means that you are tired, and tired people have arguments. Initially, there are arguments on serious issues which give way to serious arguments over minor issues, and then you end up arguing on any and every thing. The reason does not even have to qualify as an issue. There are people who have arguments at normal decibel speech; then one of them starts shouting, usually the husband. It progresses into a shouting match which could end up into a wrestling match.

That is the time when the bells begin to ring really hard. That is the time to leave, lady. Because the moment the husband becomes a wife-beater, the wife should beat a hasty retreat and call it quits. Wife-beaters as a rule, never reform. The act is almost addicting. And, the wife becomes so used to the beatings that it is pathetic to see a woman wait for more.

I talked to one such young lady who had unfortunately got divorced after the first year of her marriage. Both were working; she could hardly see her husband. (I must tell you that theirs was a love marriage.) They were working for foreign-based multinationals. The hours were so long that by the time they came home, it was past 9 p.m. Her husband came in later because he met up with some friends for a drink.

She used to know a fellow before her marriage. No, she said, he was just a friend. But he started coming over to their house very frequently and since her husband came in later, he would find her friend there already. She did not mind him because he was good company and in any case, she did not want to come to an empty house. When she asked him to stay for dinner, he readily agreed, for he was a bachelor. Her husband started to get irritated of him. Her friend would not take the hint. But after he left, they got into fights over him. Love making was then out of the question. Soon, they drifted. And it was mutually decided that they leave each other.

"So why didn't you ask your friend to stop coming over?" I asked.

"Initially I wanted to spite my husband for being selfish and staying out after he finished with his work. Then I started liking his company."

"Didn't you realise that your marriage was heading towards a catastrophe?"

"Yes, but by the time I realised, it was too late. Since there was no sexual relationship between us, the initial attraction that was there, evaporated very quickly. There were many friends who tried to patch things between us. But I had begun to hate the idea of being married to him. I knew it was a mistake. The redeeming feature was that we had no children. It made things easier."

Some one who has obviously seen everything comments:

After marriage, husband and wife become the two sides of a coin. They can't face each other, but stay together!

This happened in the olden days. They had to stay together because of the social stigma that divorce carried

and for the children which were there as a result of earlier pleasurable activities. Today, such coins are in circulation much earlier. Divorce is like going to Sunday Church. You come out of it clean and purged, and people tell you what a timely and intelligent decision you took. What is the sense in staying together if you are not happy? The oldies tell the neo-divorcee, "Darling! You already look so radiantly fresh! All ready for a new outing, I can see that!"

I asked Mrs Shamsher Singh who had been married for 65 years how she had managed to stay with the same man for so long! She had gone through multiple falls, fractures, a brain stroke and an angioplasty. Her husband Captain Shamsher Singh had shrapnel embedded in his lungs, and as a result had only one lung, had bullet injuries in the legs, and all because he had decided to join the army and then the war. Both are mobile and in the top of their spirits. In fact, I had met them as they were proceeding to the club for a party for their 65th anniversary, holding each other's hands. She said that the thought of being separated had never crossed her mind. She had a home to look after, she had to help her children grow and become responsible citizens; there were ups and downs, but who cares. They were just milestones which had to be crossed as we cross bridges when we come to them.

I asked her, "Were you a working woman?"

"Nooo!" she said, "If you have produced four children, you jolly well look after them. Between producing and rearing, where is the time? Then one has to look after other members of the family, since we had extended families."

"But, what about his faults? I bet he had many of them. The biggest being his love for golf," I prodded, "He must have spent hours away from home and you had to look after the home and the children all by yourself?"

"So what?" she said, "My biggest job was to look after him. At least with golf, he had regular exercise and I knew where he was. But mostly, he was in forward areas which were non-family stations so often, that I had got used to doing everything on my own."

So you can figure out why they have been together for 65 years.

"Fights? Oh yes, plenty of those! But which married couple doesn't have them? The fun is in reconciliation. The best love making was during those days when we had just called off a fight," she said coyly.

I noticed that she did blush rather well for a person of her age!

The great question... which I have not been able to answer... is... "What does a woman want?"

...Sigmund Freud

If this gentleman could not answer the question, then I suppose it is definitely not a simple one. I don't have the answer either, but I am sure it would not be too hard to find out… from the lady herself.

I have a friend. He is married to a beautiful lady. It was a love marriage. They have not been married for very long, but their association is a long one. My friend has been having a problem with one aspect of her psyche. I am sure if he tries, he will find many aspects. But first things first; my friend used to know a girl in his younger days, also an acquaintance of his wife. That little girl has grown since then and so has my friend. But his wife suspects my friend of being soft on his friend. Maybe my friend is. Maybe they are even ready for a little affair on the side. His wife, like all women, is very intuitive and maybe she has caught on. So she goes up to his friend in a party and blasts the shit out of her. And then she takes on her own husband and gives him a sound verbal thrashing. She has done this in the past too.

Reason: She has the best husband in the world and no other woman has a right to even look at him.

Now, I ask Mrs Shamsher Singh, "What about jealousy?"

She looked at me and said, "Yes, what about it?"

I said, "Did you ever feel jealous? Your husband is a good-looking man and maybe he is looking around? Or that other women might want to entice him into a little something on the side?"

"So let him! Who is bothered? What matters is that at the end of the day, he has to come home. Back to me! How does it matter if he has dipped his little wick into some inkpot? That never bothered me. If you have to be a mare in a long race, you have to leave these little things aside and not let them bother you. Have a little faith. I really don't know if he has ever been unfaithful. But if he intended to, then my sitting there like a hawk would not have mattered one bit. What he had to do, he had to do. Why should I be worried all the time? That way I would have become old too early in my life and died early. Moreover, what you don't know can never hurt you. I think that is also one sure way to evade an early divorce."

Give each other space... that is my advice to these young ones of today.

She continued, "But I also made it clear to other women and my husband that I frown upon such behaviour and I have a very bad temper. Thank God! I never had to give a demonstration. I was lucky."

So what do women want? First they want a good-looking husband and then they want to protect the poor little thing from the world. I asked another lady who was having so many problems looking after her blood pressure; it just did not feel like coming down. I probed some more. It took time, but she came out with it in the end. Her reason was that she thought her husband was having an affair with her best friend.

"How sure are you?"

"Very," she said.

I said, "Very is still not 100%. You should not start getting your blood pressure up at 'very', but when you are sure it is 100%."

She said, "I think, it is 100% sure."

I asked, "Do you have photographs? Because only that is 100%, or if you have caught them in action, have you?"

She said, "No."

"Then it is not 100%, is it? In any case, even if what you suspect is true, then too, it is not worth getting your BP high. So what do you want to do?" I asked.

She said, "I want to confront him."

I told her that would be foolish, because if you confront him, you leave him with two choices — either he denies it or becomes belligerent and says, "Yes! I am having an affair. What are you going to do about it? You have a home and you have your children. I give you everything, don't I? You get your sex too. If my needs are more, then I have to go out. If you don't like it, leave!"

Then, I said, that would leave you with two choices — either you leave him, your house and your children, and get ready for a long divorce battle, or you back off.

If you leave, where will you go in this big bad world? Back to your parents? After that, what? You know, men are the real predators in this world. A divorced woman is considered easy to pick. You have to live separately, fend for yourself and fend off the predators. If you are not prepared to leave after the confrontation and continue to stay in the same house, then you have given him tacit permission to carry on the good work that he was doing. So?! Are you ready to leave what is yours on a suspicion? I suggest you back off now, and cool it. No affair lasts for more that 2 to 3 years. Someone else is going to dig out the affair for you and then they will have to back off. Then you will have your husband back and a man who has to prove that nothing really happened and will behave doubly better.

And that is what she did and that is exactly what her husband did and is doing. I have no idea if he had an affair or not, but he is behaving well and the lady's blood pressure is also normal.

But what else does a woman want?

She wants the romance in their marriage preserved. He should be nice to her, bring her flowers or an occasional gift, murmur sweet nothings and make regular love to her. ***Wow! Lady, you are not even there. You are working. When you are not there, he will be murmuring sweet nothings to some other woman. He might bring you gifts and flowers, but they would not mean a thing. Lady, to run a home, the lady of the house has to be there. That is the basic requirement. Metropolitan cities are so huge that one might live in one end of the city and have an affair in the other end and no one in the world can ever know. It is only in smaller cities, like Chandigarh, that even if you fart in your house, someone in the other end of the city will tell you about the pollution you caused.***

But what does the man want?

So I asked the gentleman celebrating his 65th anniversary. He said, "The most important things are commitment to one's self, commitment to the cause, faith, respect, trust and patience."

I said, "Is that all?"

"Is that all?" he asked me, "These five are quite a handful my dear young fellow. The most important thing is the commitment. First, I have to be committed to myself, to

TRUST
RESPECT
FAITH
PATIENCE
COMMITMENT TO ONE'S SELF
COMMITMENT TO THE CAUSE

what I am and why I want to get married. Before jumping into the marriage, I should be sure of what I expect from myself, from the marriage, and finally from my wife. It would be a good idea if one knows what the wife expects from the husband too."

"Once one is sure of all that, the two partners should be committed to the marriage, that together we shall make this happen, no matter what. It is not an experiment where we say, "Okay, let's see if this works!" It works jolly well. This is what the people in the West are doing. They take up the project of marriage as an experiment. At the drop of a hat, they are ready to go their separate ways. Some of them do try to hold on to what they have. But the rate of divorce is high. Too high for comfort!

"One should accept the fact that no one is perfect in the world. I would not be too wrong if I say that everyone in this world is perfect. Only our expectations from each other make people look imperfect to the other. So if you accept each other's so-called imperfections, take the good with the bad and the ugly, if there is one, then half the battle is won. Like my wife said, "Give the other person his or her own space." Khalil Gibran said, "Let there be spaces between you. Let the winds flow between you or something to that effect." He was right, you know. I wonder if Khalil Gibran had a good family life himself. I suspect he did not, otherwise why would he have become a philosopher?" he chuckled.

"Also, if she had always criticised me for my golf, for my drinking and whatever she did not like in me, we would have made life hell for each other. Make a guess. Would we be together? We would be, but as two warriors, fighting each other, exactly like India and Pakistan. Always fighting for one thing or another, but neighbours all the same." Spoken like a true army officer!

"So," I said, "You expect everyone to be saints. There are so many couples living together and they must have the same thoughts as you have, so why all the infidelity. Why all the anger? Why the divorces? There are couples who are indulging in all these and still living happily, apparently happy, if I may add."

"No!" he said, "No one is a saint here in this world. We have our share of imperfections, like I said. We have our anger, impatience, lack of trust and all that. But what we have to learn as we go along is that we have to curb them. One of us has to succeed. I never said that both will have all the qualities that we talk about. But, if I have a temper, then she has to learn not to retaliate and vice-versa. If she was always late for an outing, I had to show patience, something I naturally lack. But, most of all there has to be a commitment to ourselves and to the cause. Here the cause is the institution of marriage."

He goes on to say, "Respect is something which is very important. The kids of today have no respect. They do not have respect for themselves so how will they respect others."

He continues, "The junior partner has to be totally respectful to the authority of the senior partner, the husband in this case. There can be no conflict if the wife is totally respectful of the husband's wishes. The husband too has to reciprocate to a large degree. Some people feel that the respect goes on the downslide as the years go by. Somewhere down the line, respect is overtaken by love which has been nurtured over the years. Respect gets overshadowed, though it is still there. Love is definitely superior to respect. And that is the time when it seems that the wife's respect for the husband has somewhat decreased. But the truth is that it has been surpassed by love."

"These days, the young married ones call each other by name. In our case, my wife has never addressed me by name. They think they are equal in the partnership. That can never be! It is all right theoretically, but not possible pragmatically. Even if the husband is junior to the wife in age, he still is senior in the partnership. It is in man's nature to be the manager. If the woman tries to undermine his pride by telling the husband that he has to wash utensils if she is going to cook, he has to wash the clothes if she has to go to work or look after the children, it might work for some time but later his natural nature will take over and he will object to the arrangement in any way he can. He can either start coming home late, or start drinking too much alcohol and become belligerent or resort to wife-beating. But he will not bury his pride indefinitely. This happens in the West. We are told how the husbands help out in the kitchen, throw out the garbage, wash the clothes and some of them even do the cooking. I ask you, if everything is so happily in order, then why the divorces. Children should be watching how their father helps around the house. They should be the ideal progeny the world has ever seen. But then this is not what we see happening! On the contrary, we see so many of these children revolting, turning against society and ending up being totally anti-social, getting hooked on to drugs, resorting to crime and leaving home at the age of 16. Now, most of them refuse to get married and have children. Women, in an effort to rise up to man's level, resort to using drugs, free sex and generally a very open life. Without realising, she becomes a plaything for the man, despite the fact that she too thinks that she is treating men in the same way. But is she? Who is the loser here?

"When our women see or hear of men in the West helping at home, they also feel that their men should be doing the same thing. They forget that the Indian men have been used to a different kind of treatment, with domestic help doing most of the menial work at home. It was an accepted aspect of a woman's domestic duties to look after the house and the children. She wants a change, but is the man ready for the change? I don't think so. That is where the conflict starts from."

To that I agree totally.

I met an army wife whose interpretation was hilarious. I asked her how many years she had been married to her army officer husband? She said 43. That was impressive by any standards. I asked her how she had managed all those years. Must have been very trying!

She said, "It was simple! I was 18 when I got married. After a few months of married life, my husband got posted to a non-family station. So two peaceful years were on the horizon! He did come on leave, but that period was just like a honeymoon. I was extra nice to him because of the realisation that he would go back after a short period. He was also on his best behaviour. And he went back, happily. Then came the children. Time passed. We moved back to a family station, stayed together and he realised what wonderful home food he had missed. The luxurious home life was great. And, as expected, he started interfering in the household and later began to realise that the family demanded too much. I also felt that he did not have too much to do. So the arguments and the fights started. And, lo! He had to leave for exercises that the army likes to dabble with, for three months. Peace! It was just letters, children and the house. After that he was back and the same routine.

And then came the wars! I have been through three wars. Those days one realises the importance of a husband, of your children and your home. Every day, it was a white sari affair, going to a new house where the officer had died. Each day, the torture of the thought of having to wear the white sari which one had kept for oneself, expecting the news any time! I would like to tell all those women who think army wives have such a cushy life… just live those 7-9 days of each war in exchange, when no army wife could sleep, no one made food, no one went for movies and for us there were no songs playing on the radio. One just sat next to the radio for the news of the war! Just worried! And hoped! And prayed! All the while, the white sari looking down on us, very ominously!

Anyway, after the war, things were nice for some months, when the two of us realised the importance of each other and the children. But then all good things have to come to an end. The fights started all over. The reasons were the same. Once again, the army exercises and the wars came to the rescue. So life passed on its own pace. Now, he is retired. He plays golf and I play Mahjong! We meet in the evenings, worry about some problem our child or the grandchild has. We have hardly any time to think about ourselves and fight. All the issues are now over. It is time to go, to move on, and not worry about the years we have spent with each other. It is a time to enjoy what we have, whatever time that is left for us.

I thought about that for a long time. A long time. Yes! We had always thought that the army personnel had a very cushy time and their wives were always having a ball. But this also proved that no matter what, the couple still had to work on their marriage and the sacrifices down the line are a part of the deal and the vows.

I asked her what she missed most by getting married.

That really started her on a walk down memory lane. She was a talented singer and wanted to do her masters in performing arts. Music, in her case! She had got admission in the University and then the marriage proposal came along. Her parents jumped on it like two hungry lions waiting for a prey. Out went the M.A., and she settled into married life at the age of 18!

I reminded her of the doha:
Kanak kanak tey sau guni
Madhakta adhikayey
Yeh payey boraye, wo khaye boraye!

Here I was substituting '*kanak*' which originally means gold with 'marriage'. I told her that in the long run, the decision of her parents to marry her off to a good man was proven right. In the present scenario, a person who does not get married remains unhappy and the ones who get married are also unhappy. It turns out to be a no-win scenario.

After some pause, she agreed and said, "Yes, you could be right. I have had a good life generally, but I really missed on the University life, the singing, etc."

I recently read that love is entirely a matter of chemistry. That must be why my wife treats me like toxic waste.

The great Indian Guru, Osho had a very different concept about love and marriage. Without delving into the entire thought process of Osho, let me restrict myself to the basics. As we know, in the Indian scenario, love generally develops in the married couples as they live their lives together. They get to know each other after marriage, since marriages are usually arranged. It is never a hit and run trial and couples are trained to get used to each other and love comes in as a growing up process, when you get used to that person being around. My friend used to say that one falls in love with one's pet after six months. Here we are discussing a human being!

One can even say that one grows into the marriage and love is a by-product of the close association. But Osho felt differently. According to him, love goes out of the window the moment one gets married. Because after marriage, the security of the arrangement takes over. The law comes in as the saviour. Because, the partners begin to think that if one of them thinks of opting out of the arrangement, then he or she is protected by the law. The beneficiary in this arrangement is usually the woman, for she is considered the weaker of the two. She is protected for the future by the thing called 'alimony'. So, when the law, like the sword of Damocles comes into it, love has to go out. This is more relevant in today's scenario where pre-marital interaction between the couple is very evident. And they marry after they think that they have fallen in love. Osho's theory of love going out of the window is not relevant in the old Indian scenario where the couple did not even see each other before marriage. Love has not seen the light of the day yet. So love departing out of the window does not seem right. But most of the marriages in India are still the arranged ones. Here, love is not in question. It is just a matter of basic rights of women.

Most human beings do not even know the basics of love. For them the physical attraction is love. The famous American singer John Denver is a living example of friable love in a community where the term 'love' is used so superficially. It is a just a figure of speech for them. Most of the time they use it as a mouthwash, to take the bad taste out of their mouths. Or they throw the line, 'I love you' after a person, as a parting shot which hits the backside of the person for whom it was intended, instead of the lips.

John Denver, in my opinion, wrote the most beautiful song ever penned, for his wife Anne, and it became an instant hit and still remains to be one. But only as a song! It was called Anne's song. Either John Denver did not mean a word of it or it was meant to convince his wife as a last ditch effort which did not succeed, because they divorced two years after the song hit the stands! Funny, isn't it? Most of the developed societies of the world marry after a courtship period, unlike the Indian scenario. These days, they live together for a period of time, get a look at each other's bad habits, decide if they can survive them and once both parties are convinced that love is in the air and they are meant for each other, only then do they decide to marry. But things go sour very strangely. Naturally as the gentleman said, love is a matter of chemistry and their chemical reactions go bad rather hurriedly and the husband ends outdoors; later, followed by separation as in Denver's case.

I had a talk with my German friend Deiter Grathwohl. Grathwohl has stayed in India and Pakistan for many years, countries which specialise in arranged marriages. He had gone through a divorce and ended up with a couple of fatherless children out in the wilderness. So I asked him what led to the divorce after being in love with his wife.

"You loved your wife, didn't you?" I asked him.

"Sure, I loved her!" he said. He felt that his marriage had restricted his personality development. This affected him so much that he decided to opt out of the marriage. After ten years of restricted personality development, he decided to tie the knot again, to a lady who had also opted out of her first marriage. Maybe for her personality development! Now that their personalities had developed, they were better suited to wedded life. Grathwohl had since become an accomplished artist, though he was completely untrained in that field. He now created exquisite metallic frames for his paintings, which were truly unique. One could call them his signature frames. The thought of painting had never crossed his mind while he was in his first marriage. Now he was a hunter and also fished to his heart's content, when he was back in Germany on vacation. He had also become an avid gardener and a golf-lover. Quite a lot fills his kitty, won't you say? Do you feel that he had a point there or was he plain selfish?

I asked him why there were so many divorces in his country and his answer was thought-provoking. Fifty years back, women were not so educated. Their primary aim was to look after their home and children. If they divorced, they had no means to look after their children and had to lead lives of servants. Then girls started going to colleges and the universities. They got jobs and became self-sufficient. If they did not like life in the marriage they were in, they simply decided to leave. The change is more in women than men.

India, now, he said, is in the stage where Germany was 50 years back. Though girls in the metropolitan cities are studying and taking up jobs, the proportion is still too less. Majority of Indian women in India are still not self-sufficient to start living their own lives if divorced. Socially, they are not accepted. They move around with the tag of a divorcee. So these women will carry on accepting all the tortures dished by the husband and his family.

I said that the male is responsible for not letting the female personality develop and not the other way around. He begged to differ. He said men have to do a lot of things and perform great deeds. The woman hinders his progress. I said that there are a lot of German couples who have lived many years together and have no intention of divorcing. He agreed and said that these men have reached their comfort zone and have no further desire to improve their personalities. So they settle in a groove… in which they are comfortable. Then they settle down to rearing children, getting them settled into jobs and then wait for them to get married. Soon, they are old and they can do no better than do what they are doing.

"Me," he said, "I can't stick to just one thing. I have to do many things. So, now we have four weeks away from each other. She goes back home, does her things and I do mine. These days I paint."

So I asked him, "What is the secret to your happy married life now?

He said the same thing, "Give each other space."

We go to the restaurant two times a week.
A little candlelight dinner,
soft music and dancing!
She goes Tuesdays,
I go Fridays!!!!

"So are you happy now in your marriage?" I questioned.

He made a face and said, "Yaa! I have been a very unlucky man in marriage. **I left my first wife and this one won't leave me!"**

And, he brings out thick guttural German laughter.

Then why do people in happy marriages, peck on others?

"Nature!" he said, "Nature! Man is like an animal. He always wants to improve upon the generation that he has already produced."

I said, "Man doesn't have extra-marital affairs to produce more children."

"Yes!" he said, "But it is in his nature to produce more. And with different ones he can do that. The only thing is that society won't let him produce more in an extra-marital situation. In any case, in an affair, man can't produce children but he carries on with his obsession with other women because of his instinct to improve his generation. The natural instinct is always there."

So I said, "What about the woman? She also has extra-marital affairs."

"She also has to improve her generation, the same way that a man has to. It is woman's nature too," he said, "In the western world today, women don't want to get married early and if they do, they don't want to produce children. In the metropolitan cities of India, the trend is catching on. What they forget is the fact that children are the binding force in a marriage. If that binding force is missing, it would automatically lead to more divorces."

I asked Deiter if I would be right in saying that people would gradually settle in a groove and marry later in life.

He said, "Maybe! The chances are that she might not get a healthy male to marry, but the desire to produce children will always be there. It is nature."

I told him, "Children produced by matured women may not be healthy. The incidence of diseases in these children is more."

"Yaa, yaa," he said.

I changed the topic. I asked him, "What keeps the marriage brimming?"

He said:

1. ***Whenever you are wrong, admit it.***
2. ***Whenever you are right, shut up.***
3. ***Always remember your wife's birthday.***

   I asked how that is possible.

   He said, "All you have to do is to forget it once!!"
4. ***Forgiveness is important. A good wife is the one who always forgives her husband when she is wrong!!***

He then dropped the bombshell, "Indians are bisexual."

I said, "What?"

He said, "Yaa, yaa! When they get a woman, they are heterosexual. When they don't, they are homosexual."

I looked at him, amazed. I always thought there were more homosexuals in Europe!

"There are," he said, "But percentage-wise, the population of bisexuals is more in India because of your population."

So I asked, “Where are the children coming from?”

“Nature! The nature of man is to produce children and then to improve upon the generation! When that is done, after the age of 30 or 40, they change.”

I asked again, “Only Indians?”

He said, “No, no! All men are like that.”

My mind went to that lovely lady who once came to my office and I raised the topic of marriage. Not my marriage to her; only for discussion!

She said that I should go to Delhi and see what is happening there. They have Thursday clubs for homosexuals and Saturday clubs for lesbians. My eyes had opened wide.

She said, “Haan! 40% of the married population of elite Delhi are homosexuals and lesbians! At least in the circle that we move in!”

I said, “Whoooa!”

When I narrated the story to another friend, he said, “So why are you surprised? Why go to Delhi? Go to this restaurant here in Chandigarh itself, and you will see boys in lipstick mooning around with hulks and on another day, see the lesbos in action.”

My eyes opened wider. “Whoooa!” I said again, “Where am I? Hibernating, of course!”

Then I asked Deiter about the importance of sex in a married couples' life. "How important is it to hold the marriage together?"

"About 40%," he said.

I said that according to my calculations, it is not 40%, but almost 90%. I gave him the quote:

If the woman keeps the man adequately satisfied sexually, he will be like a pet dog and he will not have to foray into garbage dumps.

If you see a happy couple, you can safely bet your life on their happy and fulfilled sexual life. See a couple which is always quarrelling, and then too you can bet on your life that they are having a horrid sexual life. Even if people quarrel, a happy couple will always make up in bed. A golden rule to follow is never to let a quarrel overflow into the next morning. The bed is the best place to start a dialogue. Who starts the patching up is immaterial. It has to be over before the sun is out the next day. A lot of times, ego in partners makes things tougher for the couple to decide who will take the first step. Hence, one of the partners has to bury the ego very deep, preferably, into the neighbours' yard.

But in India, that cannot happen. You see, women are relatively inexperienced in sex. Ours is a very depressed society where women are kept behind closed doors. The only person she can ask about sex is her mother or her friend. Both do not know enough.

The mother will say, "Oh! It is nothing. Takes a few minutes of your time! You are supposed to just keep making a lot of sounds and act as if you are enjoying the process. Actually it has nothing to do with enjoyment. Maybe the man enjoys for the last fifteen seconds or so. Then you will get a child and that would be the end of it for a few months."

That is exactly what she has been doing. And that is what her mother told her about the wonderful act of sex. After all, Madame Alka Pandey has just come out with her version of *Kamasutra* in relation to women in the present times! However, not all women, mothers and girlfriends will read the book. Even perusing through such a book in a bookstore will generate a lot of eyebrow raising. Men will automatically do a 'two plus two is six' and form an opinion about the woman's sexual libido in the bookshop itself.

The friend has no idea what she is talking about because she has never done it herself.

But, I say, girls these days know a lot about sex. Everyone is reading about it, seeing erotic magazines and blue films. And they are doing it with their boyfriends even before marriage. So they have to know.

But these few do not constitute India. The rest of Indian women do not know much, that I can tell you.

Also, the Indian male is an oaf. He has no idea about foreplay and what pleases the woman. He has no time and nor does he have any inclination to find out. For him, it is still the same old WHAM BAM! THANK YOU MA'AM!

Ho! I say, hold it! Remember, we wrote the *Kamasutra*! We are the world leaders in the theoretical aspect of sex!

Deiter maintained, "Theoretical knowledge is different from knowing it practically. Also one must have the will. Here, the man will come home drunk and throw himself on the woman. The woman is already subjugated, so she will not resist, knowing what to expect. She knows no better. That is why I am saying, in the Indian context, sex is only important for 40% of marital success."

"And, the rest of the 60%?"

"That is mostly dependent upon the woman — how well she looks after the man's requirements, how well she serves him, how well she keeps her eyes and ears closed. I am not saying that the woman does not need sex. She definitely needs it but then so much depends upon the quality of sex available. If it has to be a drunken outing for the husband, then the woman might even give it up or look for it elsewhere."

The lady who finally took a lover was heard saying that if she knew that a lover is such a good performer compared to her husband, then she would have taken a lover much earlier!

"The reason behind this statement is that the lover has to be adept in the art of love making, because he would get a repeat order only if his first performance is outstanding. For a run of the mill performance, the husband is enough."

"Wow!" I said, "You do have a poor impression of the Indian male."

So if what Deiter was saying is true, the argument and the fights will last longer than required. Because, the male has no concept about sexual diplomacy!

Once, a husband was waiting very impatiently for his wife to come to bed. He had visions of a great night. As his wife came out of the toilet after changing into 'something more comfortable', she bumped her knee on the table.

The husband was up immediately and enquired, "Darling, I hope you didn't hurt yourself on that ***stupid*** table?"

After everything was over, the wife got up and walked towards the toilet and bumped the table again, louder this time. The husband was very irritated. He shouted, "I know you are ***stupid***! But are you blind too? Can't you see where you are going?"

This sums up all. Where would we be in the absence of sex?

My wife and I agreed before we got married that when an argument arises, one of us must take a walk in the forest to avoid problems and further aggravation. Ever since, I am living outdoors!

I told Deiter that in India, we have a saying that if there are utensils in the house they are bound to clang sometimes. As a consequence, if two people are living together, they are bound to clash. So making up is the most important aspect of a marriage. If the cold war persists too long and too frequently, then the message that goes out is that if this is to go on and on, must we live together?

Deiter, busy smoking his pipe, repeated, "Ya, ya! This is the life!" He does this very frequently, without really being philosophical.

Then suddenly, he brought himself back and said in his slow drawl, "Yes, yes! It is natural that two people argue. But in marriage, there should not be too many. It is not good for the marriage."

So I looked at him and asked, if one of the two should always be on the receiving end. That if there is a joint family, like we have in India, then the wife will always be the one who has to keep quiet — first, in relation to her *saas*, and then to her husband. So, is she the persecuted one?

To err is human. But to blame someone for your problems is strategic.

There is a Chinese fable which is repeated more often than one realises. For some reason, I feel that the Chinese were very mature and intelligent as a people. Their fundamentals were very clear. If we could read up the Chinese way of living, *The Tao*, quite a few of our problems would be solved.

The fable goes like this:

There was once a pretty-looking woman who got married. She was loved very much by her husband and was spoilt thoroughly by him. On the other hand, she had a torrid time at the hands of her mother-in-law, or she thought she did. She realised that she could bear it no more and thought of methods to end her misery. She reached the conclusion that if the mother-in-law should die, that would be her only salvation. She went to a chemist who dealt in herbs and intimated him with her predicament. The chemist, after thinking a lot, agreed to give her the herbs which would kill her mother-in-law slowly. But there were conditions. Since the poison was slow-acting, her mother-in-law would be very ill during that time, so she would have to be extra nice to her and agree to all her wishes and commands so that no one could suspect her. The lady agreed reluctantly.

She made soup from the herbs and was very obedient and nice to her mother-in-law. The old lady noticed a change in her daughter-in-law and started being very nice to her too. Over a period of time, their relationship changed. One day, the daughter-in-law ran back to the chemist and asked for an antidote for the poison. She told him that she no longer wanted her mother-in-law to die because she had become such a nice person and she, in turn, had begun to love her. The chemist then revealed to her that he had never given her any poison in the first place. The herbs only contained vitamins which the old lady needed. Now she was healthier because of the love and looking after that she received at the hands of her daughter-in-law.

There was a happy ending to the story but the moral is that if you are nice to people, they will also be nice to you. This is all the more relevant to the scenario of marriage, be it your husband or your *saas*!

It is just the question of seniority and respect. In this case, the mother-in-law and then the husband. We don't want to discuss the role of father-in-law, because this gentleman is never expected to take part in frivolous family matters. He comes in only when there is an emergency. After all, one day, the daughter-in-law will become a mother-in-law herself and then the seniority would be hers. So why be in such a hurry?

But one very important lesson that we learnt from the Chinese fable was that love and respect has to be mutual. So the mother-in-law has to respect the daughter-in-law as a human being and a new entrant to the family. She should also understand that being the wife of her son, she is an integral part of the family. Moreover, why expect one

person to adjust to so many people in the family. Why can't the rest adjust themselves to the new entrant?

The million dollar question is that why the mother-in-law always has a running battle with the new bride. After all, it was she who looked so frantically for a bride for her son. It was she who so happily arranged the wedding, trousseau and the initial welcome. Then what happened? I have seen it all. I have treated mothers-in-law for sudden cardiac symptoms, dyspepsia, migraine, backaches and so on. Of course, the daughters-in-law dare not have any of these ailments. These are reserved for the senior lady. Why does she develop insomnia? Not to forget claustrophobia, if the newly married couple lock their door for want of privacy! Suddenly, she cannot breathe if their door is locked. What does she expect? The door should be open wide and she should be able to hear all the wonderful music? Every small thing that the new lady does has a niggling irritant effect on the mother-in-law. If she enters the kitchen and keeps the matchbox in a place which is fairly visible, but not where it used to be, heaven help her!

How dare she take over my kitchen… did I hear the words correctly? Now it is 'MY' kitchen! It is announced that she should be able to find everything, including the salt and the mustard sauce, with my eyes closed! She forgets that they had never bought mustard sauce before!

The daughter-in-law dare not change the location of any curio that has been languishing in a vague corner for years. The mother-in-law likes it exactly in the place it used to lie in. It gives the corner a character of its own. These upstarts think that we do not have the vaguest idea of interior decoration. And, I have been doing this for donkey years. The house was running fine… till this one arrived. Nothing seems to be to her liking.

The daughter-in-law is already petrified of stories of mothers-in-law passed on from one generation to the other. Then, one fine day, the newly married couple decides to go out for a dinner, or an after dinner stroll, or a coffee somewhere. She will be shocked to find the grumpiest woman in the world awaiting her.

"No one tells me where they are going anymore. No one takes permission any longer. When my son wasn't married, at least he would tell me where he was going. Now, he too has been affected. Your getting married doesn't mean that I have stopped existing!!!!"

Then she comes up with the best of them all. "I have never been insulted so much in my entire life!"

Tears of the size of snowflakes come pouring down her cheeks! To a new-comer, it would seem like it is really the end of the world. The son and his wife look at each other and then at the father-in-law. He has no idea what to do about it. After many recurrent episodes, he suggests a trip to the psychiatrist or their family doctor.

"Yes! Yes! This is the last straw. Now I have been declared mad by my family. Now I have to be taken to the mental hospital. I will give you a better suggestion. Give me a little poison and polish me off! The very root of your problems will disappear! As such, I am of no use to anyone. Now that this one has come, you won't need me?

"Hai oye rabba! Why didn't you take me away from this ungrateful world? I have been working my butt off for this family and suddenly, I am redundant. They want me to go to the psychiatrist so that they can officially announce to the world that I am mad!"

Then one day, the tantrum will be on the sob side. There will be bucketful of tears and no one is wise enough to understand the reason WHY.

The daughter-in-law looks at the husband with tears, obviously. The son has understood the picture. So he tells her to forget it; she will soon be alright. Most Indian families have similar stories. If there are other siblings, they too join in the hate campaign. But if the reason for all these tantrums is only the feeling that the new girl has taken away my son, then it is fine. These will be skirmishes with pauses of peace. But if the reason is dowry or the inadequacy of it, then things can get really messy.

Anything is possible, if the son is not strong enough and does not give his wife ample support. Or if he too feels that he could have bargained for more and that he has been cheated out of his rightful share, then he too adds his bit and it could end very very messy.

Reasons for the conflict can be never-ending. Most of them have no locus standee. But in families, these reasons have created so much stress that marriages have ended in total chaos. Some have ended with the newly married couple running away and staying separately to earn some peace. I am sure these couples would be wondering if the decision to marry was a good one. This is also the reason why so many of this generation are deciding to stay away from the joint family system. They are ready to break out on their own and dump the support of the family. This is also the reason why so many young people are not marrying.

But, enough of all the bullshit! The mother-in-law works up all this venom for just one reason. She just cannot stand this little girl snatching her baby boy from her. Why, till yesterday, it was, "Mummy! Do this for me, do that for me. Mummy! I want this and I want that." Before doing something or going some place, he would ask her if he could do that or go there. Now, all of a sudden this witch has done some kind of a magic on him, and all that love and dependence on her has just evaporated into thin air. She just cannot fathom out all that. She cannot even call her home ***her home*** anymore. She has to share everything with this new entrant. Even her husband dotes on her, like she was someone special. She is no longer an entity in her own fiefdom. What happened here? She can see only one enemy and she goes after her with all the guile she can muster.

This is a problem of the modern times, when people don't have too many children. They have only eyes for one. But in the families of orthodox *banias* and their allied class of Indians, the bride, no matter how educated she is, she has to stay at home and run the kitchen.

The question of people having expectations from each other is the area where so many feuds begin. The wife is expected to serve bed tea; she is expected to be a cook, a hostess, a perfect partner in bed, a perfect mother and finally a perfect wife. Most of the times, the wife does achieve what is expected of her. But heavens help her if she is ill or has a shortfall in any one department!

On the other hand, there are a few expectations the wife has from the husband and mind you, to the feline mind, these are of paramount importance. For example, tiny demonstration of emotions, like love, respect and sharing. Naturally, men fall short on all these. Always! It is in the initial few years that he tries. As the years pass along, the sharing and expressing of emotions become a thing of the past, something of a dream, of which he has a vague niggling recollection. He is not sure if there was something in his past life. Yes, it must have been in his past life. Like I said earlier, sex also becomes mechanical, predictable, devoid of any feelings or enthusiasm, totally lacking in variation or imagination.

When the wife looks for some real romance, the husband would ask, "Are you crazy? Are you really expecting all these things to happen? Be real, woman. Thank your stars that something is happening here!!!"

However, women, being the more sentimental of the two, get hurt here. Nowadays, when they foray into the corporate world, there are hundreds of predators waiting to shower praises and give her all the romance she is looking for. When they have had their fill, they just move on to another woman looking for the same things. And, there are so many of them!

There is an old joke on this:

I was running across the park and came across a man jogging nude.

So I asked him, "Why are you doing this?"

He said, "All your fault, man! All your fault! You came home early."

First guy (proudly): ***"My wife is an angel!"***
Second guy: ***"You are lucky!***
***Mine is still* alive!"**

Indians are notorious in marriage matters. They treat their wives like punching bags. Agreed that most of them begin to look that way, but seriously, you cannot take everything literally, can you? Top of the pedestal is the dowry issue. The Indian husband is considered the best catch in the international female circle, because he is timid and is considered very much a family man. He does not have affairs and tends to be value-oriented. This is true only in the international scenario. Because the dowry issue has no base in foreign countries! It is only in India that this takes up a draconian character which goads Indians to beat, maim and burn wives. There are countries where the prospective husband has to pay a dowry to the girl's father. Even if we as Indians consider those people backward, it is noteworthy that nowhere in these cultures will the father of the bride beat or kill the groom if he cannot pay the required dowry. It is just logic. If he does not have the dowry, then he does not get the wife. Simple!

Why can't that logic be used in India? If the girl does not have the dowry, then do not marry her and do not bring her into your house. Here, they marry the girl and bring her into their house, keep what she has brought along as dowry and then begin to harass her to get more. If she cannot oblige, heaven help her! If the man discovers later that he cannot get enough out of his wife's father, why not simply divorce her? Why harass or burn her?

There is a different angle to this. They burn the poor thing and pocket whatever was given by her parents. And then the man is ready to marry again!

We are truly unique. The funny thing is that the whole family gangs up on the hapless woman. Here, the parents and siblings of the husband will join hands and use their collective imaginations to find ways and means to break the newly wed bride. If she does not commit suicide herself, there is plenty of help at hand.

The first step is to get rid of all the help (read servants), for a new unpaid one is now at hand. All eyes zoom on to the new bride. She cleans, she cooks and washes the entire dirty linen. If she survives all that, then things start in earnest.

It usually begins with snide remarks which graduate to taunts. This could be in relation to her physical attributes. Nothing is right for them. Then start the taunts about the dowry. If the dowry is enormous, it will naturally end up with, "Your father is so rich but see what he gives you? This is just a pittance! What did he think we are? Beggars?"

So the message goes across that the dowry is not enough.

Basically, the dowry is never enough. Recently, the dowry issue did not spare even a very senior police officer's daughter, who had spent a huge sum on the wedding and gave a large dowry. That marriage definitely seems to be having a downhill course!

Here I must say that these are mamma's boys who have no idea what self-respect is or what happiness means. Do they think that by going through with this charade, they themselves would be at peace and happy? What can anyone achieve by collecting a few more household articles or some more money in the bank or maybe get a car by twisting his own wife's arms? That too, from a person who is supposed to be your life partner. What kind of respect is she being offered here? What will she think for the rest of her life, or when she is in bed with him? She would be thinking about the car, man! What kind of emotions will this man evoke in his wife?

Please do not forget that Indians have a tradition where the wife pops on to the husband's pyre and tells her dead hubby that she is in on the ride to heaven or wherever else he is headed to. This happened only in India. A few cases have been reported very recently too. *Sati* began in the olden times when the enemy attacked and if he was sure to win, then to avoid being raped or carried off by the victorious army, to be used for nefarious purposes, the wives of the defeated warriors used to jump into a community pyre. And if the dead husband was brought back from the battlefield, she still joined the hot party. Was it all voluntary or needed a lot of coaxing from the senior women of the community is a point which can be hotly debated till the cows come home. Nevertheless, *Sati* had become a tradition, where all the women in the state of Rajasthan were expected to do just that. Little girls were persuaded to dip their hands in progressively hotter water so that she could get ready for the eventuality. Raja Ram Mohan Roy decided to end this practice, though it continues to exist in many of the remote corners in the country.

Have you ever heard of a man jumping into the fiery funeral pyre of his wife? Never! Because, the husband did not fear rape by other women if their own wives died. Whatever you may say about the tradition, it still required a lot of guts to jump into the fire! The dead do not feel pain. On the other hand, the lady is alive and kicking. She would definitely feel the heat. One wonders how long it took the lady to reach a stage where she stopped feeling the heat and pain. Modern Indian mothers-in-law have taken it upon themselves to keep the tradition alive and merrily continue to burn their daughters-in-law. Only **difference is that** the husband is not dead yet, but the wife soon is. Oh! Don't these mothers-in-law just love fire?

Cool it, man! Don't you know that when a person gets married, his life changes completely? His priorities in life change. The inhabitants of the five circles which surround us change. When we were young, our innermost circle consisted of our parents and us. The siblings were in the second circle. Friends and relatives were in the third and fourth circle respectively, and finally, society filled the fifth circle.

But when a bloke gets married, his innermost circle now has him and his wife, replacing his parents. When they have children, they take up the second circle and the parents are relegated to the third circle. Finally comes the fourth circle where the man's siblings reside. Society and relatives live in the fifth. If any man is fool enough to keep his parents in the first circle even after he is married and accepts the destruction of his own and his wife's happiness at the behest of his dowry-hungry parents, then I would be forced to say that I can do nothing but pity this guy. He should not have got married to begin with.

I happened to meet a young man, belonging to the state of Haryana. His family is from a place called Sirsa. Pretty backward guy, I thought. First of all, the common opinion about Haryanvis is that they are traditional to the extent of being backward and if someone belonged to a place called Sirsa, then he had to be ancient. But when he got talking, my eyes kept widening as time went by and my ears became sharper. By the end of all, I had developed exopthalmos. (To the uninitiated, it is an ailment in which the thyroid gland starts working overtime, making the patient's eyeballs get pushed out progressively, till they are almost out.) Mine were like that after spending some time with this man who called himself Siddharth.

He had been married for a short time and had a 3-month-old son. He said, "You will be surprised to know that I had never seen my wife before my marriage.

Neither had she. Mind you, I am a product of a public school in Delhi. But there are certain traditions that we follow in our family. We do not question our elders. That is rule number one."

"My wife's father had told my grandfather, that he had brought this girl into the world as a respectable person and not someone whom he would put up in the market for marriage. If you want her as your daughter-in-law on the strength of my family, then it is fine, otherwise you can go and look elsewhere. There will be many more offers for her."

"My grandfather brought home some sweets and told my mother, 'Oh bahu! I have said yes to your future daughter-in-law!' That was it. Mind you, my mother was no illiterate woman from the village; she herself was a retired bureaucrat. She accepted her father-in-law's dictate. I asked him if it was a good gamble."

'Couldn't have been better,' said Siddharth, 'She turned out to be a post graduate from the University and a gold medallist! And even if she had not turned out to be good-looking, I still would not have complained. You see it is a tradition.'

"We have other traditions in the family. We make our father realise that once he comes back home, he has come to his fiefdom, where his family would be waiting for him to come back from work. His wife would wait with a glass of water, something to munch on, and clean clothes after his bath. When my father comes home, if the T.V. is on, it is switched off. You see we make him realise that his slogging during the day for his family is worth it. That we care for him! I have never countered his word. What he says is a command which has to be agreed to without argument."

While speaking at an award ceremony where Sethi was being conferred the title of the Citizen of the Millennium by a group, he returned the award saying that he was not deserving enough. Addressing the gathering in his native Haryanavi, he told them that they had no identity of their own. Living in cities, no one knew them and no one cared. They were just some people living in flats where the neighbour was not bothered who they were. They did not know where the wife was, where the husband was, where the daughter was and where the son was. And frankly, no one in the family cared where the other was. Even if they were sitting in the house, each was locked in his own room, doing his own thing. When the father came home, no one even got up to offer him a glass of water. He was just another member of the group they called 'family' and he was contributing just as the others were. Hence he was treated as the rest. You have to make the father feel the head so that he acts as one. I can say that I worship my parents. How many of you sitting here can say that?

At this point of time, I can tell you where my wife would be, where my mother would be and what they would be doing. Can any one of you, sitting in this big city, be certain of where your family members would be at this moment? A lady in the audience said that he was very conservative. He replied that having respect for each other is not being conservative. Being thoughtful about the 50 odd people in my extended family is not being conservative. Knowing who enters my house is not being conservative. Making your parents proud of you is definitely not conservative. Making my father know that he is respected and his word is a command is again not being conservative. Eating together is not conservative. Being moulded into a family unit is not conservative. Worshiping your parents is not conservative by my book. It might be by yours. Definitely not by mine! If this is conservative, then I would rather be conservative!

So he tells me, in a household like mine, how can we think of clashing with each other? There can be no thoughts about a divorce because there would be enough seniors to counsel the couple. And finally, since their word is a command, the quarrel has to finish, sooner than later.

That is when I changed my opinion about Siddharth.

But like I said, there has to be respect in a partnership and the respect has to be earned to some extent. I say some extent, because in the Indian context, a certain amount of respect is already his by virtue of his being the husband or the senior member of the relationship. Can you imagine this lady respecting her husband despite his behaviour? I doubt it. So when the base of a relationship is so fickle, I can see it heading in only one direction. Down!

This marriage survives even if it is unhappy, because it becomes just an arrangement where the husband and wife live together not in a symbiotic relationship, but because the man has to propagate his species and has a home where he gets all the comforts, children being looked after and of course, as they say, availability of any time sex. He has the sex cheque book, doesn't he?

Indian marriages have an in-built cheque book function. Any time the husband wants sex, all he has to do is tear off a leaf.

This is what happens in most Indian families. But with educated women coming out of universities, getting jobs and earning money, they are more aware of their rights. They are less scared of ending an unhappy marriage into which they are stuck just because they had no other way out.

The point is not what women want as Freud asked. The question here is:

WHAT DO MEN WANT?

If they carry on doing and behaving the way they have been doing for centuries, there will be a time when women might not even marry. Some are already asking the question —

GET MARRIED FOR WHAT?

Some of them do not even want children.

CHILDREN FOR WHAT?

There are many women in the world who have decided to suppress their natural instincts of motherhood and decide not to have their own. Instead, they have begun to adopt children. Their sexual preferences have changed too. They do not want the problematic heterogeneous relationships and are opting for same sex relationships, which they think have lesser complications.

I asked a few women, "What will happen to the world if there are no children being born?"

"Who is bothered?" they say, "There are already so many children in this world who have no place to live and nothing to eat. It is actually a sin to produce more. Moreover, it is not my responsibility to carry mankind forwards. There are still enough foolish women out there. And if I ever had the urge to have my own child, I would look at artificial insemination!"

Man is basically a selfish creature. He wants everything whatever is good in the world for himself. He needs a home where he is looked after well. And a family, (because that is his natural urge… to father a generation and then to let the wife look after the children)! But society has thrust certain unwanted duties on fathers for some centuries now. These include getting them educated, settling them into good jobs, and finally getting them married. So he is more or less stuck in this arrangement. I think, he is beginning to enjoy this.

He needs his drink in the evening. Some need to improve upon their generation, as suggested by Grathwal by having extra-marital flings. He has a roving eye by nature, but he understands that he has to look after his family in more ways than one. Sex seems to very important for him and he goes through his life, worrying about the time when he will cease to perform. Basically, he is a simple, weak-hearted, insecure human, whose need to have a woman looking after him is more than the woman's need to have a man to look after her. It might look the other way, but take it from me, he needs her more than she needs him!

Right! Now, enough about men and mothers-in-law being the culprits! Women are also to be blamed. Traditionally, men have been slogging it out and earning money to look after their families. They never bragged about that aspect. You have to hand it to them here.

Women who earn money have one motto!
My money is my money.
Your money is my money!

But then, women started working, and some of them earned more than their husbands. These upstarts, as I refer to the ones who earn more than their husbands, cannot keep their tongues under control. At every opportunity, they will remind their hapless husbands about the money ***they*** earn and how ***they run*** the house. It is not that they ***contribute***. They do not have that word in their dictionary. When they go on a jewellery or shawl buying spree, the husband dare not interfere because it is her money that she is spending. The final dialogue that clinches the issue is, "You should be buying me all these things, you know. Here I am spending my own money and still you object."

What do you think the husband wants to do here? Obviously, he wants to burn her. Since he cannot do that without his mother in the Indian setup, some of them start beating them up, just to show the lady who the boss is.

What should the lady do?

If she earns more than her husband, she should learn that it is a symbiotic relationship, where the husband is the senior partner. There is no way his pride could be undermined. If a man's pride goes missing, it is the end of him as a man. There is a direct relationship between a man's control over his sexual prowess and his self-respect. He should be made to realise that he is still the person running the house. The woman is the homemaker and the man is the one who runs it. Despite the fact that she earns more, she should massage his ego and pride. This will ensure that she is respected too. Can't the man buy himself a Rolex watch, since he earns money too? But if the two of them start buying their own extravagances, I really have no hope for the marriage. Hold it, ladies! I am only trying to save the marriage here. If you don't like what I am saying, trash it, but not before giving it some thought!

I am very sure there must be a lot of ladies out there who would be calling me an M.C.P. But ladies, it is a tough world out there. The sooner women realise this hard fact of life, the happier they will be in the marriage scenario. What the hell, I was not the one who manufactured marriages! I am the one who got married 33 years ago. If this had been an Amazonian world, things would have been different. You could have turned men into your slaves, raped them, even gang raped them. You could have beaten and maimed them, maybe even burnt them. But then, it is still an old fashioned world, no? Just act as if you are the second in command, all the while knowing that you are the captain of the ship!

And, what does the man think of his marriage: There is a way for transferring of funds which is faster than e-banking... it is called marriage.

You ask any woman if sex is important in marriage and she will say, "Of course, it is important but only to a limited extent. The main things are the understanding between the two, love, respect and trust."

One tends to get very impressed by such dialogues. But in real life, the story is a bit different. The man remains sexually active for 30 years of his married life and wants his activities to be fairly, if not hugely pleasurable. However, Indian women are not really interested in sex after the birth of her children and during their growing up. BUT! But, if the wife discovers that the husband cannot make love to her because of exertion or some ailment, then God help him.

Her tongue goes on over drive. At every opportunity, she will remind him that he is hardly a man. Sorry, I beg your pardon. It is not 'hardly a man'. He is NOT a man!

She will shout her lungs out at every opportunity, "He can't even get it up. Something which every other Indian can do without any effort! We have the population statistics, don't we? Even animals can do that. Has anyone heard of an impotent animal?" She really socks every unwilling listener by telling about her *kismet*, to have a husband with this malady.

If she gets in a tight corner in a gathering because of her husband, she is ready to publicly announce what her husband can and cannot do. Is it not an incentive for a self-respecting man to kill the lady? I bet it is. But don't even think of killing. It is inhumane and illegal. Divorce her? Yes, yes! But does every impotent husband divorce his wife? No! And, why not?

There are a whole lot of men who gladly or otherwise take it lying down, just because a tiny part of them is non-functional in relation to a person who is not interested in it in the first place. Why? For the sake of dear home or because he is too old to fend for himself. He actually needs her or has convinced himself that he cannot do without her, at that point of his life.

I knew a respectable man who had married late. His wife was still very presentable when his little associate decided to call it quits. His wife had still her hormones running at full blast and in fact she quite liked men. Towards the fag end, she used to bring home a rich man she had befriended and entertained him while her husband slept in the adjoining bedroom! I don't think the man slept. Did he contemplate suicide or other drastic measures? I bet he did. But the hapless bloke copped it before he could put his thoughts into deeds.

But I have asked myself this question many times. Why did he continue to live through the ignominy? He knew that his sons and daughters-in-law knew all that was happening. Why didn't he leave? He had the money! So why didn't he? It would be easy to call him a gutless coward. Reminds me of a song sung by Kenny Rogers "Ruby, don't take your love to town". It is about a war veteran paralysed below the waist in the war and he pleads with his wife not to leave every evening to seek favours elsewhere. Since she pays no heed to him, he expresses a desire to take his gun and put her into the ground, if only he had the power to walk to his gun.

On the other hand, we know of many so-called respectable husbands who have pushed their wives and daughters into prostitution. What does one call them? And we have definitely got mothers who have pushed their daughters into prostitution. The permutations and combinations go on and on. We know of wives who have enough of their husbands' sexual advances and then they push their daughters to their husbands. One need not forget the daughters who get involved with their fathers so that they can get favours from them. What about the famous men who have forced their sons to send their wives to them? It is a wild world out there!

The so-called sacred institution of matrimony, as it is, has fallen by the roadside.

So I asked a woman named Komal, who has been married for 27 years. I said, "Why does a lady do that? Why, after years of good times does she behave like a you-know-what?"

Prompt comes the reply, "Control! Just a matter of control! She just wants to control her husband, and what better way and timing?"

"And why does she want to control?"

"Nature," she said, "It is in woman's nature to control. Just as the man has been controlling the woman for so many years and she meekly accepted subjugated existence. But that was just a way to keep the peace in the family. However, once a man becomes technically impotent, she sees and snaps up the chance to control."

Then the man understands that if given the chance, his wife is going to open her oral trap bigger than the great white shark. So in a gathering, he carries on being a henpecked husband, taking care not to say or do anything to infuriate his wife and activate her tongue and vocal cords.

All his life, the husband has been drinking himself silly at parties, making an ass of himself, ignoring his wife's entreaties. Now, all that she has to do is to give him a stare and down goes his glass. Earlier, she had to put a gun to his head to make him go home. Not any longer! One glance is sufficient to send him scurrying towards the door.

"Haaa!" I thought, "So wives want their husbands to become impotent in the later years of their marriage for a whole lot of reasons. First, she has the control, second, he does not force himself on her anymore, and third, his roving eye will automatically become sightless as his libido becomes toothless! She is no longer embarrassed in public."

You must have heard of the Indian saying "A man never grows old. He only loses his balls!" And there is another one "Men are like horses! They never grow old!"

What I am getting at is simple. Okay, okay! I know! Not all women do that. But, I insist that in the larger majority, this is what happens, at least in the Indian scenario. Is it a natural thing or are they forced to suppress their desires? Apart from the menopause thing, they tend to lose their way and put on so much of weight that the callisthenics and the athleticism involved has no attraction for them anymore.

But the male is still active. What should he do or rather what should the wife do? Allow him his discretions and look the other way, without making a big hullabaloo? After all, she has had a taste of what he has to offer for many years and I am sure his performance must have gone down the hill too! In his case the desire is still there, but the flesh is feebly willing! So, what is there to lose? Is jealousy justified? This is a point you have to debate yourselves, when your mind is at ease. I had an opportunity to discuss this with a friend of mine who has been married for 50 years.

I asked him bluntly, "How have you stayed married for 50 years to the same woman? Were there times when you wanted to call it quits? "

"Many times! But at this point of time, I don't consider her my wife any longer. She is only the mother of my children now! I haven't had sex with her for the last 20 years. We just live together!"

So I asked, "How did you manage going without?"

"Oh! You have to make yourself understand. And if the urge is too much, I was always self-sufficient. Weren't we all? From a stage of self-sufficiency, we went on to a stage of dependency. And then making the circle complete, we come back to the stage of self-sufficiency."

I looked at him oddly and he said, "Didn't we all begin our sexual life with masturbation? That was what I meant by self-sufficiency."

And, I let out a long *aahaaan* of understanding!

A spouse is someone who stands by you through all the troubles that you would not have had if you had stayed single.

In recent times, many jobs have been created where the man can work from home, which means that the husband has his office at home. Naturally, the wife, being a lady has a heightened aesthetic sense. So she has the chance to come into his office and sit around, looking all over the office, beginning with the ceiling, going round and round, till she reaches the unreachable areas. Mind you, the man is working! She then gets up and drags her fingers over the table, looks at it, smells it; then she succeeds in penetrating holes and crevices which even they themselves did not know they existed. And then she will study the outcome with as much seriousness as a scientist on the verge of a world-shattering discovery. By now the man has lost all interest in his own work. He no longer knows if he was working in the first place. He is looking at his wife and her discoveries. She will then raise her head, look at her esteemed husband and announce, "How dreadful! This place is full of cobwebs and dust. How can you work here?"

"So where else do I work from? Should I leave the house?"

"Nooo silly! I meant that at least you should get the office cleaned once in a while. What is Ramu here for, darling?"

With that, a shrill scream will erupt from the deepest recesses of her throat, filling the whole neighbourhood with a sense of doom. It will sound something like 'Raaaaamooooo'. This is her servant's name stretched to its limit. It is actually Ramu.

These days all Ramus are short of hearing and then the whole house starts reverberating with her 'Ramooooos'!

Ramu does not come but the neighbours start hollering, "Since Ramu won't come, should we come instead?!"

The problem here is that the husband has stopped working, Ramu is not coming and the wife is not leaving. The husband, finally, has had enough. He does not know if he is coming or going.

He commands his wife, "You are not to enter my office. If I need you here, I'll call for you, though I doubt very much if the need will ever arise."

But then women are women. She will come back again and again, uninvited of course. Is this sufficient ground for divorce? You bet it is. The man has to work, hasn't he? But if you look at it from the wife's point of view, you will understand that she is not just exercising her vocal cords. She could be doing something better. She has your best interests in mind. Working in a dusty atmosphere could easily give you the sniffles. You then would lose out on your working hours and if you convert them into money lost, it could turn into a mind boggling sum if you earn by the seconds.

The husband realises that there is no way he can find peace at home, and so he walks out and goes to the bar. There he sees a saying behind the barman's station. It says:

Those drinking to forget, may please pay in advance.

Everyone else, excepting me of course, is convinced that wives are nags. You probably look at them with coloured vision. They do not nag you just for the heck of it. They have your image in mind; they have your health as a priority and want you to preserve your wealth for your retired life... and theirs too!

You don't believe me? See, if you drink too much in a party and begin to make an ass of yourself, she is worried about your public image. That is why she keeps reminding you not to drink so much. But with your ear plugs so tightly wedged inside your ears, you can hardly hear her on normal levels. Never on the first take at least! As a result, she has to repeat herself again and again and the decibels have to be higher. You mistake her intentions. All eyes are already on you. When you succeed in achieving the exalted status of a party ass, she sacrifices her own fun at the party by bestowing full attention on you and your actions which could easily be misinterpreted.

She has then to tell you to behave yourself and stop pinching the backside of the lovely lady in red. All that while, you are having a bird's eye view of her neckline which suddenly makes your eyes lose their power to blink. This is despite the fact that the lady in red is loving the attention. All of a sudden, when the D.J. starts off the hip-vibrating music, you sweep the lady to the floor. You, who are normally such a good dancer, suddenly get converted to a driver in the children bump car arena. My dear fellow, please understand that it is embarrassing for your dear wife. Just put yourself in her shoes and decide if the announcement of a sudden headache and desire to go home is justified or not.

There is never any intention of berating you. It just seems that she is too busy exercising her vocal cords. If you overdo the eating and drinking, and you put on weight which is terrible for your health, what else can she do? You do not listen on the first go, ever. So she has to keep reminding you. You behave so childish at times. Did I say

'at times'? Yes, I must have. Actually, most men behave childish all the time. They just do not want to grow up!

Didn't your mother ever scold you or remind you that you have to brush your teeth before going to bed, or you should not keep putting off your trip to the toilet and to please stop crossing your legs if the urge gets too much, or stop farting in public? Just because of your childish behaviour, you bring out the motherly instincts in her. What else can she do? Think about it with a cool head.

All wives are backseat drivers, some more and some less. If she is sitting on the pillion seat of your jazzed up motorbike and you drive like there is no tomorrow, and if she is nervous enough to cause pressure sores on your right shoulder, or when she starts giving you instructions to apply brakes or change into a lower gear, if you forget to do that when you are driving at 20 kilometres an hour in the fourth gear, or when she has to keep telling you to turn right or left even if you know the whole route like the palm of your hand, you should never lose your cool. She is just trying to help.

There are wives who want their men to grow up and be matured and not stay a mummy's baby. How will your personality blossom? So if she wants you to get away from the constricting effect your mother has on you as an individual and the two of you as a couple, she has to keep telling you to break out on your own. Don't call it nagging because you are the one who won't listen! Look at it from her point of view. First she is nagged by her own parents... do this and don't do that. Then the husband, meaning you! Now, now, get that holier than thou look out of your face. And then your mother! She is just sandwiched between you and your mother. And, when your children grow up, she has to listen to the same things from them. Do not forget your daughter-in-law if your son is married. Just to prove that she is not a bitchy mother-in-law, she goes overboard with her daughter-in-law. Now she has to cater to a shouting son, nagging husband, overbearing mother-in-law and the dove-eyed petrified daughter-in-law. And you call yourself the persecuted one! So what is the harm if she says that she wants a house she can call her own in this lifetime? I knew it! You don't agree with my point of view. At least the lady will!

Don't you criticise her cooking, her appearance, her lack of time management and the fact that she is never on time for anything. If the party starts at 7:30 p.m., and she invariably starts getting ready at 8 p.m., it should be expected. She does not want to reach the party before the waiters have arrived. And in any case, if you arrive too early, the hosts would think you had nothing better to do. Most of the time, the hosts themselves start getting dressed pretty late! She just does not want to embarrass you. And if you reach the party too early, you tend to drink more. Never mind the fact that, while waiting for her, you have already finished your third drink and are ready to sleep. Remember, acceptance is the trick. No sense in going to a party in a foul mood.

If you had to go for a movie and she is finally ready when the movie is about to end, please ignore because this is what she has been doing it ever since you were engaged. At least you were able to see the end of the movie! That is what the whole movie is all about. THE END. The rest of the movie is just leading up to what you have managed to see. Haven't you been nagging her to be on time? Did it affect her? See, you should learn from her. Why do you get into a flap over such a petty issue?

Take life as in the long of it. If you have been married for 40 years, that makes it 21024000 minutes. So if she has been late for even 10000 minutes out of that, she was still on time for 21014000 minutes. Now isn't that something to think about? Always take the larger picture into consideration. Now you can safely adore your wife's punctuality.

Then we have these ultra-modern couples who are bored within the confines of their marriage and say, "Agreed we took our marriage vows and till death do us part and all that, but there has to be some degree of excitement in the marriage. Let's do something which brings the zing back into the relationship!" So, they enter the wife swapping experiment. Out go the 7 *pheras* and all that. Suddenly they derive 'excitement' from different partners. The permutations and combinations are so many. The husband is happy because adultery has a new meaning now. It is legalised within the marriage framework, and there is no guilt. Understandably, they are no longer husband and wife. They are in an arrangement where they are only living together. Meanwhile the level of depravity reaches newer lows as they experiment with newer ways to end their boredom. The marriage has already ended.

PART 3

Children

Were we not told that children will only be legal if they come out of wedlock? That means that the reason why most humans married was to procreate and produce children with valid legal standing. If we forget about those women who do not get married for one reason or the other, suppose the ones who did marry and then refuse to bear children! The man marries because he wants children and unfortunately, gets landed with someone who does not. Many a times, the opposite happens, that the wife wants children and the husband does not. These are strange circumstances. If both stick to their guns, it becomes a stalemate. Something over which they will continue to try to convince each other initially and then argue over the issue and then finally there will be a day when they will throw in the towel and call it a day!

We would not spend too much on those who have called it a day. We will talk about the normal ones who have married and then gone ahead and had their kids in the normal fashion. No matter what one might say but I feel that the best things that can happen to people, which make them immensely happy, irrespective of how they end are — getting married and then becoming parents. They begin to look after their children with such single-minded dedication that to an observer, the thought of that couple having problems in future life is next to impossible. When they have so much to share and love, the thought of quarrelling or divorcing is a very difficult thing to fathom.

A very important issue that arises in these circumstances is the value of a coach. In all games, we have coaches who tell the players how to hold the club or bat, how to hit the ball, etc. The Indian cricket team is the only team in the world which does not need a coach, though they pretend that they desperately need one. But when they get a coach, their performance goes down!

But in marriage, there is no coach. In fact, there can be no coach! There are people who can give a few hints, but there is no one who can be called a master in this art of marriage and rearing children. Parents are there but they too got married at a young age, produced their share of children and brought them up to the best of their ability, committing their share of mistakes, sometimes practising hit-and-run techniques. They can only share a few tips with their children, but there is no guarantee that they are right. When no two humans are the same, how can the children be same? We just cannot use the same mantra for everyone.

You too will grow in this institution of marriage, commit blunders and probably learn. And then, you might not! Times are changing. What was right a few years ago is wrong today. What you thought was a complete no-no, is something that everyone expects the children to be doing today. The dilemma would naturally be — how should children be reared?

I raised my children on Majoral, the baby aspirin and gripe water. Today, the doctor looks at you with murder in his eyes and heads for his gun, if you mention the word 'Majoral' or 'gripe water'. I sometimes wonder if Majoral was not there, how I would have gone through the hundreds of fevers my children decided to suffer from. Thank God for small mercies! They have grown into fine adults.

This is how my wife and I learnt. I am not saying that we were always right or always wrong, but our children are now grownups with their share of complexes. Some of them have been contributed by us and some are their creations. They will blame us or thank us according to the situation they are in and to their convenience. I can't bet on the thanks though!

But no matter what, children are truly heavenly creatures! When they are to arrive, even the differences between the *bahu* and *saas* take a backseat during the waiting period. The arrival of children is such bliss for everyone that everything else is forgotten. The daughter-in-law is sadly nudged into a crevice of false hopes.

Now imagine the scene if a girl is born when everyone else was expecting a boy! Whoo and whoosh!!!!! It could be curtains for the hapless mother.

And if a girl of the family, in her excitement, asks the mother-in-law what was the outcome, prompt comes the reply, "What did you expect? Another of your kind has arrived." As if she herself was a male!

The venom in her voice could easily stun, if not kill, any old proud Anaconda or a Boa Constrictor from ten feet. The tension could be great enough to decapitate someone if he tripped on it.

An impartial observer would have been probably numbed by the response of the mother-in-law. She is probably looking at the two daughters that her elder son has and the two daughters that the younger son has. So for her, the arrival of another girl is the end of the world. But woman, the girl child has arrived into your other son's house, not yours! It is their first child and to them it does not matter either way. A boy is as welcome to them as a girl. In fact, to some, a girl is more important as a first child.

But the mother-in-law has to have her way. She has to screw her daughter-in-law's happiness. Her son has no say in any case. As time will pass, this same woman will dote on the girl. She has no war with the child. She is just a weapon against the daughter-in-law!

Basically parents are great. They are not born into greatness but by a quirk of fate, they become great almost instantaneously. One moment, they are husbands and wives like any other human beings, trying their best to be perfectly miserable, quarrelling over petty issues and non-issues. The moment ***their*** child enters the world, everything changes. The wife who could not forego her beauty sleep, could not do without her bed tea, her shopping stints, her kitty parties and her social circle, is now a changed person. She can hardly sleep because of the wailing, ever hungry infant who is alternating between passing stools and urine and demand to be fed. But that does not bother her one bit. The smell emanating from these products does not bother her either.

The thought about socialising hardly enters her mind. Kitty parties are a thing of a distant, forgotten past. There is no interest in sex. The young wife, who wanted a drink or two in the evening or that smoke, will not even think about it and all because of the detrimental effect it might have on the child!

The husband is a changed man too. Always ready to pluck a leaf out of his sexual cheque book at the drop of a hat, now would not even let the hat drop sometimes! Now he is ready to help out, with caring for the baby, changing nappies, warming milk for the child or washing and boiling feeding bottles, humouring the baby by producing indecipherable sounds and most of all, ready to sacrifice his sleep.

Most of you who are parents must be going back into time. Put the book down and imagine what you felt when the child was born or when it produced sounds like 'maa ma' or 'paa pa'? Or when it took the first step or even put the spoon of food into its own mouth on its own, for the first time? Did you run for your mobile camera or your camcorder? I bet you did. Did your eyes become moist when he or she got admission into the school where you wanted it so desperately to go? I bet they did. When the sports day came, you were out in the front with your camera, heedlessly blocking the view of other parents by your enthusiasm, despite warnings from the school authorities to lie off? In the annual day celebrations, how the dances graduated from the fairies to the yoga and finally to the bhangra! The subsequent events were landmarks.

A few years later, another child arrived. Did your enthusiasm reduce the second time around? Definitely not!

No two children are the same. They bring with them different habits and idiosyncrasies. The thing to ponder over is what happens next. In the olden days, mothers went on looking after her brood, till her dying day, that is. The father had other things to do, so he did other things, like bringing food on the table. Some of them realised that their cheque book was no longer valid because his wife was not interested in encashing it any more. She was more than happy with the children. Thus the husband had no other alternative but go to another bank!

The scenario is different these days. Once the children are old enough to fend for themselves which means that they have crossed the stage of crawling, the mother suddenly wakes up to the fact that she has put on weight. As such, breastfeeding the children is a big no-no. That activity destroys her sex appeal. The forgotten gym activities, her kitty parties and her social circle beckon her like mermaids. They rise from the dust like the phoenix. Like dazed sleepwalkers, they have their arms extended in front of them, and they walk straight into the arms of their kitty members or their gym instructors. The shopping malls suddenly loom large and they lose themselves in the maze of the lingerie stores and the plush movies theatres.

The children suddenly discover nannies. As they grow older, they are banished to boarding schools.

The problem here is that there is very little attachment for their progeny if the mother is a working woman. This statement will be contested vehemently by the mothers. They will most probably be screaming at me at this very moment, "How can you say such a thing, you dirty old man!"

But it still is a fact that she treats her children like interfering pets if they ask for too much attention. Doesn't she have to work? Doesn't she get tired by the time she is home? The mother's role too has its limitations, no?? If she has a social group, automatically there are kitty parties to attend and the children will be in the way. She has two options. Either she hands them over to their nanny and scoots off to her pals or she just packs them off to a crèche.

When the husband comes back from office, they have to attend to guests or become guests themselves, no? They also have to have a life, you know. Please remember, these are the same children whom the couple doted on. When they come back home from wherever they went off, they produce those lovely sounds, "Oh, come here my little pooch. Mummy missed you soooo much!" Bull shit! Even the kids know she is lying. "Oh my baby! Did you miss mummy?"

The kids look at each other as if saying, "Are you for real, mom? Give us a break, mata! What do you think?"

If the kids are off to the boarding school, the affection lasts till they are nicely ensconced in the hostel environment. The instant that moment passes, the parents heave collective sighs of relief and quickly go back to where they came from, back to their beloved routines. When the children come home for their vacations, the same coochy-coos are once again heard, but by now the children become self-sufficient. How much they require their parents for emotional support is anybody's guess! The more important thing is the material and financial support. And, do not forget the pocket money!

When you ask these children once they are all grownups about how much they missed their parents, they will say, "Oh hugely! Now, when we are at home, we spend quality time with each other!" Which means that the parents do their thing and the kids do their thing! They get whatever they want since they are home for a short while. There are chances that the family does things together for some time, at least for appearance sake.

For some, the very children who gave them so much happiness, become stones around their necks. There are incidents reported recently that women go into depression, collect their brood and jump into a river or in front of an obliging train to end their lives. Then there are men, who for some reason become so frustrated that they have slaughtered their wives and their children in the most primitive manner.

These are the same people who were so happy when they got married and even happier when they became parents. What happens with time? Why do they take out their frustrations on their children and respective spouses?

This needs some delving into. Another WHY!

This brings us to two important issues — parenting and the effect on children. We have successfully dealt with the issue of marriage, why some people marry and others do not, why some of them stay married and why others decide to call it quits, why some parents have children and why some decide against having them.

Obviously, the next point would be to find out what makes some couples great parents and some lousy ones. Also, why some children turn out to be such wonderful human beings, an asset to society and why some become terrors, nightmares for the world at large!

People these days are so good at coining big words. They no longer call each other mad or retarded. They say 'mentally challenged'! If someone cannot hear, it is no longer 'deaf'; it is 'hearing impaired'! Things used to be so simple in the olden days. Now they just want to make things complicated. These days they call bringing up their children in the good way as 'Positive Parenting'. As if parents in the past were practising negative parenting! How many understand them and how many succeed in implementing them in their lives is a different question. Who even has the time?

The joint family system of India makes all the difference between parenting in the past and parenting today. There was such a vast network of family members who gave the child a feeling of being bonded in the family. It was a support system offered to the biological parents. They had an option open to them in case both the parents wanted to work. The child had no problem of being lonely. The grandmother, grandfather, uncles and aunts were foster parents, so that even if the child missed the mother, there were so many people to look after it, till the parents returned. Those days one rarely heard of kids jumping into wells or from four-storied buildings or an obliging train comes up to knock them to Timbuktu.

If you ask anyone what he or she would like to have in this world, they will say happiness, almost immediately. But hasn't everyone made their own lives unhappy by running after materialistic things, hoping that those will give them instant happiness. Dude, all that was required of life to make it happy was a little oxygen with a dash of carbon dioxide, food and a cave to live in or maybe share it with a bear or a lion. Whatever! But then we went on to invent the wheel and look at the mess we are in. We want more and more of everything that we already possess... more cars, bigger cars, more houses and yet bigger houses; one wife does not do the trick either, have to have more women.

Anyway, that is already done. No one can go back into time. These are the times when couples work. They do it so that they can provide a better life to their children. Are they successful? The parents are never there to be a part of what they are working so hard for.

The staple dialogue of children when they grow up is, "Mom, you were never there when we needed you!"

The mom is shattered. Here she has worked her ass off for these children and this is what she got in return! There is no gratitude in the world these days!

I think my mother hated me; she got morning sickness after I was born!

But this works two ways in negativity. If you do all what you do, the children say that the parents were never around. But in case the parents are not in a state to provide all the goodies that the kids desire, then the dialogue is, "You could never give us anything and you were never there for us either!"

They say even if you come first in a rat race, you still are a rat.

Like I said, when the children become older, the parents want to do their own thing. They fail to notice that their children do not want them around. Since the favourite dialogue from the parents is 'don't do this and don't do that', which the children just do not want to listen to any longer. They would rather have their own friends and pass time in a group which understands their problems. Suddenly, the parents realise that the years have flown and their children are all grown up. They want to be included into their world but then it is too late. The children have already reached a stage of no return.

They have already started doting on their peers. They get so dependent upon them that they forget that they have parents too who could give better advice. For them, the advice that comes from parents is the same old unintelligent 'do this, do that, don't do that' advice given to them in their childhood. So they do not even ask. The peer effect is so much that they tend to latch on to their habits as well. So smoking, drinking, and drug usage depends upon the peer group effect. If their seniors and friends partake all this stuff then it is alright for them too. Sex, crime and violence are also an offshoot of such dependency.

I have had a talk with some children who were later found out to be drinking, doing drugs and into crime. They could camouflage their thought process so well that it was almost impossible to guess what they were doing. The girls were better at deception.

It is not that all children are into anti-social activities. There are children who are hugely intelligent and who are doing so well in their studies and later on in their jobs. They are the real doers. We have all praises for them and their kind. The problem is that the percentage of the other group is so high that one wonders why they do not take the toppers as their peers. Why must they always go after the baddy group?

The questions that linger on are:

- Do they think that they are superior to the generation of their parents or even that of their elder brothers and sisters?
- Do earning money and getting materialistic benefits outweigh all other considerations for them?
- How important is family to them?
- How important is getting married?
- How important are children?
- How important is sex before marriage?
- Why do modern generation children become so enamoured with crime and quick money?
- How serious is failure in exams for them and how should the parents deal with it?

Let's face it. Children are different these days. If I go back to my teen days, I can remember the shock that I got when I got to see my first tape recorder. I was 13 years old and could not fathom for the life of me how that revolving tape could produce such beautiful sounds. My friend's father had brought it from the States. So he called all of us to his house for a tea party and then demonstrated that marvellous gadget. I was presented with my first transistor radio as a prize when I passed my 10th exam in the first division. Today, it was in the papers that this student asked for the latest mobile phone after she passed her 10th exam. This happened after a time gap of 43 years. The difference is that her photograph was in the newspaper and mine was not. My transistor radio costs Rs 800, while her mobile costs Rs 20000! In this generation, all children get what they demand for.

This is just an example. Some parents must have bought their children cars or scooters or motorcycles. In my case, it was much later that I owned a tape recorder. If I remember correctly, I had already become a doctor by then. We went at a slower pace than children and youngsters of today. They have a head start. They start pressing buttons when they are toddlers.

Accordingly, they expect to be treated differently. Most likely, like adults. The problem arises with their parents because parents are not ready for the change. Children have changed, but not their parents.

The other day when a young father asked his 6-year-old son what he had learnt in his computer class in school, the son, to his father's horror, promptly pressed a few buttons and logged on to a pornographic site. The father tried to act unaffected. He calmly asked him who taught him to do that. The son promptly said, "My seniors!"

"And how old are your seniors?" the father enquired.

"Oh! Some are 7 and some are 8 years old!"

So, the gentleman ventured one step ahead to find out what his son knew about the site. The son said, "They are just naked people (*nangey log*)."

The father asked, "And?"

"Bus! What else?" said the son.

My doctor friends were over from America and I asked them about the sexual knowledge of the young in the States. They said that most youngsters think that oral sex is not sex. This was a change after Mr Bill Clinton's testimony! Everybody thinks that only penetrative sex is sex. So, they can be seen indulging in cunnilingus in schools or wherever they are comfortable and still not be ashamed or guilty.

As it is, they used to kiss any and everywhere! And their kisses were not of the garden variety. They were the soul-searching ones which were deep. For them, kissing lips and kissing a penis and vice-versa, is no different.

I remember, my friend living in England, used to come to stay in Chandigarh with his family every year. He had a British wife and two lovely children. One year, the daughter who was about 18 that year, showed me her tongue. Right in the middle of it was a metallic bead the size of a pea. I wondered what purpose that bead served. I have had, on occasion a single hair on my tongue and the effect was so unnerving that I had to remove it, no matter what. It was so irritating! And, this girl had a metal bead on her tongue, a screw penetrating it, secured with a nut on the other side!

And her father turns around and asks, "Darling! How on earth do you kiss your boyfriend with that thing there?"

The daughter turns around and says, "No Dad! It doesn't bother us at all! My boyfriend has one too. The only problem is that when we kiss, there are a few balls clanging!"

And everyone laughed their guts out. I was embarrassed, for some reason. I was an outdated dad there. In the Indian scenario, we do not discuss these things with our children, least of all with daughters. I would have been appalled had I known that my daughter has a boyfriend. Kissing?? Having sex??? I would have hit the roof and the result would have been a BANG! He is six feet under, and I am in lock up.

But that was ten years ago. Today, I would probably have reacted the way modern parents should. Am I sure?—Take a guess!

And how should modern parents react? We know that children, as in infants, begin to discover their sexuality very early in their lives. Parents actively try to prevent the playing around with their sexual organs because the act embarrasses them.

When I was a child, my father was so stingy that he did not give me toys. I was lucky that I was a boy, so I had something to play with!

As children grow, they discover the difference in each other and begin playing their doctor-doctor games. It is but natural that they progress with the physical discovery as time goes on. But when girls grow up, they have the inbuilt shyness quotient which prevents them from carrying on their doctor games. Some of them discover other girls, differences in breast sizes and other physical aspects. Though they are not gay in the parlance that is normally used, it is just a matter of discovery of the pleasure aspect of the human body. Boys do that too! But in the present generation, the shyness quotient is rather low while the attraction towards the opposite sex is high. Moreover, having boyfriends is the commonly followed norm.

There was a small boy who asked his father the usual embarrassing question, "Dad! How did you come into this world?"

Dad says, "I was dropped off at my mom's home by a stork."

"And dad, how did I come?"

"Another stork dropped you off at our home." Dad was feeling mightily pleased with himself till then.

"Why dad, was there never a tradition of having sex in our family?"

The moral of the story is that the generation of today knows what is happening. Our job, as parents, is to have a frank discussion about sexuality and sex, the act, and the ramifications thereof when asked. You would be surprised how little they actually know. Knowing about the organs involved is different from knowing about the complicated diseases that can be transferred by the act, the moral aspects of surrendering too early in life, the possibility of pregnancy, the loss of reputation for girls and so on. Some of these children are inquisitive about all these aspects and have so many questions. We have to be ready with truthful answers.

There are others who think that they know everything there is to know and so do not ask. This attitude then gets them into trouble. There are unwanted pregnancies, the visits to quacks for abortions which could lead to complications. Even if they go to qualified doctors for abortions, these are such hush up jobs that if something goes wrong, they cannot even raise a hue and cry. If at all parents do not know the right answers, then they should be referred to someone who knows. But under no circumstances should they be given cock and bull answers.

Another aspect of this problem is that children respect their parents but they do not respect their thoughts. They find them too vintage and feel that they have a right to argue their points. But if you as parents refuse to get into a healthy discussion and persist with the same dictatorial habits, then there is bound to be a conflict of interests. *You will continue to call your children ill-mannered and they will continue to call you primitive non-communicative idiots, who also double as their parents.*

The modern clothing or the lack of it has facilitated in their discovery of each other. The free use of alcohol and stimulating drugs help in that direction. The frequent change in partners or having multiple partners is also a regular feature in their lives. I really don't think that they care about what society thinks of them. Society chooses to save face by looking the other way. But the funny thing is that when married people have extra-marital affairs, society still frowns. This often leads to divorces because one of them complains. But if the youth of today have multiple partners, no one minds. This is probably because no one is complaining.

I have a beautiful statue of Lord Ganesha on my desk. It is one of many that adorn my clinic and house, for I am very fond of Ganesha statues, mainly because there are so many poses that He is found in. This one is a very unique for it is a five-headed Lord Ganesha in the *tandav* pose. In each of His hands, He has a deadly weapon of war, and in one, He holds the tail of a snake whose head is under His foot. But one hand is raised in blessing. Whenever I look at it, my eye catches only the hand raised in blessing. I feel I am forever blessed. Automatically, the urge to touch His feet in reverence is overwhelming. One sees the other arms only with a bit of effort. Ever since I started on the chapter of children, I began thinking in terms of Lord Ganesha trying to crush evil in the world, all the while bestowing His blessings on us.

Are we, as parents too supposed to keep a tab on the bad habits of our children and crush them as Lord Ganesha crushed the snake? Or are we supposed to take them as modern day changes of society which are bound to affect our children too, and accept them, all the while giving them our blessings? This is a tough one. Remember, no one these days accepts physical punishment. After a point of time, they might even retaliate. We have examples of that already, though not too many, yet. Thank God for small mercies.

In the Indian scenario, our thought process is still primitive. Caste and creed matter so much. The gulf between parental thinking and the thought process of their children is so wide that it will take some time to even things out. Even when Indians migrate to foreign shores, they do not let their children marry into a scenario of their own choice. There have been instances of honour killings. How can any parent or sibling kill his own because of a difference of opinion? Here in India, there have been instances where parents have broken off with their daughters for marrying without their consent. So great was their anger that even after 30 years, they did not relent, despite the fact that they lived in the same city. How can this behaviour be justified?

And if children have friends of the opposite sex, can you imagine the furore that will ensue? Hence any chance of the youngster coming to the parents for guidance on sex is next to impossible, because the father will shout "Sex?? How dare you bring that three letter word into our family?!" So what do you think children will do here? Obviously, they will do what they want to, all the while making sure that parents are kept in the dark. Do you think this will foster a healthy parent-offspring relationship?

This is one set of parents. The other set is the kind that will agree to everything that their ward demands. From designer clothes, footwear, watches, mobile phones to the costliest mode of transport. For them, friends of the opposite sex are a healthy aspect of growing up. Maybe they are! When I asked Mrs Malhotra about infatuation, she heaved a heavy romantic sigh and said, "Oh, how heavenly infatuation is! I feel that every one should have at least four of them." I quickly gave up!

But these children, who have everything, have no idea about discipline. Their evenings begin at 9 p.m. and end anywhere between 2-3 a.m. They naturally get up late. If their parents are working, then chances are that they would not meet up with them.

Going back to my school and college days, we were supposed to be back from wherever we were by 8 p.m. There were no arguments on that issue. After all, what could we do after that? There were only movies. When we did go for movies, it was a family outing. I remember how much we enjoyed going to movies; Moby Dick and Mughal-e-Azam are still fresh in my memories. Sex-oriented films had not come into their own then. Fast food joints were not in vogue and spending money on ice cream parlours and the like were a big no-no. One had to live within one's means. We also knew that if we were late, Mom would be at the gate, waiting.

There is an oft repeated statement which I think is still true:

The family which eats together, stays together!

We ate together. There was no T.V. then, so today's attitude of picking up your plate and eating while viewing your favourite programme was not possible. Mom was a homemaker and stayed at home, making cakes and other delicacies for us. She waited for everyone to come home and discussions about the day were reserved for the dining table. That was also a time for her to tell us how she passed her day. Activities were planned for the next day and so on. But today, no one sits for food together. Dad is too busy at office or at the club (if the two have not left for their kitty dinner already), the children will ring up to tell them that they are having dinner at a fast food joint with their friends. So if Mom is home all alone, what can she do?

As children grow older, the present trend is to leave the house by 9 p.m. and come back at around 2 or 3 a.m.! What they do, where they go, how much of alcohol or substance abuse is dabbled in, is a point about which there are no answers coming from the young ones. In effect, there is no parental control any longer. It is a matter of sheer luck if children listen to parents. There are a few parents who compliment themselves and say that if proper '*sanskars*' are imbued into the children, they will never go wrong. People, just keep your eyes and ears open and you will never repent. I know such wonderful-looking children who lead Jekyll and Hyde lives.

It is difficult to fathom how these families will ever interact with each other and maintain a healthy level of communication. Is communication only a parental requirement? Have children no use for them as long as their materialistic and financial needs are met? Are friends so important, despite the fact that they have been with them since morning and every day? What makes them react in this callous manner?

It is not just in matter of eating together. A very dear friend of mine has two lovely daughters. I was there when they were born and have seen them growing up. Suddenly, on a recent visit to them, I noticed the elder one in a pair of jeans so tattered that any old vagabond with a healthy self-respect would instantly reject them. But this lovely lady of 18 was socialising, going to the market, attending tuitions and going to college in them with as much pride as I would have, if I was sporting a Rolex watch. I could not help myself.

"Nikhaar, why do you wear these lovely, tattered jeans?"

"Because I like wearing them," and as an afterthought she threw another reason, "Also because Dad hates them!"

"You wear them because your Dad hates them? He has a right to hate them. All through, he has been dressing you up as a doll and suddenly you decide to wear rags."

"Yes! I saw them in the Levi's store. No one looked at them but they appealed to me. I am making a statement here, Uncle!"

"What kind of statement would that be?"

"That, I am different!"

"But you are different. There is no other Nikhaar in this world. You don't have to dress like a beggar to prove that you are different! So what do you expect your father to do?"

"He should shout at me. The least he can do is to show that he is angry with me. That he cares!"

"Will you stop wearing them then?"

"Nooo! I like them, don't I?"

I look at her trying to fathom whatever is fathomable. But she looks back at me so sweetly that I give up.

I have a small aquarium in my clinic and it is placed in such a location that I can see the fish swimming all the time. I am fascinated by them. They are untiring. And, we call ourselves superior evolutionary products! We run for

half-a-mile and we have to rest. We have to eat the whole day long and these fish take in the minimum of food and swim through the day and night. Anyway, that is not the purpose of talking about the aquarium. I wanted to tell you about the tiny fish that my secretary put in. This little one goes like a shark after the other goldfish, 10 times their size. It keeps them on their toes or should I say fins, all day long. They do not attack it. They just avoid it to save themselves the nibbling. The little one, meantime, is relentless.

I got thinking about these fish, especially the little one. It reminded me of our children. They keep nibbling at us and keep us on our toes. We keep trying to understand them but they seem to be one step ahead of us. We, as parents do not bite them, but with a little bit of practice, we try to steer clear of direct confrontation. In this avoidance, do we lose the respect that they have for us? Just like that tiny fish would have desisted from its activities had the larger ones shown authority! Is this what Nikhaar wanted to tell me?

Then the father, who is also my friend of 30 years, comes home. It is late and he realises that Nikhaar has an exam in electronics the next day. So after a little chitchat, he says, "Nikhaar, kindly go to your room and study for your exam!"

Straight comes the reply "Dad! You know. No one can force anyone to study!"

1
Z
A
5
0
FAIL

We did not know where to look.

The children today are highly talented and intelligent. The newspapers are often filled with the excellent results of classes 10 and 12. One is impressed. These children are outdoing themselves. Imagine getting 100% in 3 subjects and getting 99.7% aggregate! It seems unachievable. At least, we could never have done that. The news goes on and on, about the ones who had achieved superlative feats. Then come the results of competitive exams like the IIT and the IAS. Fantastic! These boys and girls excel and do wonders. I know that the future of India is in safe hands. But then the wandering mind goes to the yesteryears. Children had scored well even then. They had become doctors and engineers, IAS officers, bankers, and gone abroad to excel there too. But then why hasn't India improved? This is probably not the right place to discuss that aspect of the country, so we will leave it at that.

But my mind did go to the ones who did not do well in these exams. What of them? Does anyone think about them? Does anyone show any concern about their future? What will they do? The ones who have failed can appear another time. They might improve their percentage. But what about the ones who have passed, but with percentages which will keep them away from any course they had planned, prevent them from joining the college of their choice, bar them from the stream they intended to join. For them their world comes to a standstill! In the euphoria of the ones who topped, the world banishes the losers to a fate which has no beginning. Do you expect these children to be depressed? Do you expect their parents to be depressed? You bet they are. Has anyone paid any attention to the children or to their parents? No! So what are they doing? Both are hiding themselves in the remotest corners of their homes. The parents vent out their frustration and anger at their wards. And mind you, this tirade is never-ending. Just the sight of them will trigger a never-ending shouting bout. This will include allegations of being let down, of being shamed in the family, city and the country; that they have no place left to hide their faces, and all through the year you kept saying that your tuitions were going very well, self-study was at the peak. Then what happened? Where did the marks disappear? What will we do now? Spend another year's money? You should drown yourself in the nearest handful of water.

Some of the children just do that. If they are too big to drown in a handful of water, they jump in front of a train or jump from a four-storied building or take some poisonous stuff. What do the parents then do? Neither do they have a scholar in the family nor do they have a child! All they can do is to cry their hearts out.

Recently, we came across a news item wherein the mother of a girl studying in class 10 was reported to have committed suicide because her daughter had supposedly not done well in her exams! When the result was declared again, it was found that it was just a misconception; the daughter had in fact done very well. But now, there was no mother! What had the mother hoped to achieve? Even if her daughter had indeed fared badly, so what? There are many years ahead of her. But now, when she is dead, who is supposed to rejoice in her success? It could even be that like parents of today, she too had sky-high expectations from her daughter. Maybe, she knew that her daughter will do well but that was not well enough for her!

So what should these parents do? To begin with, they should realise that there is something wrong with their ward. They should start searching. Look for an addiction. Look for reasons for their child not being able to study well. Is it an affair? Is he straight or does he have warped tendencies? Is he a normal child with just poor learning abilities or does he have a different aptitude? Berating never helps. In this era, where there is paucity of children, having a slow learner is better than having no learner at all. There are parents who become very frustrated because they have such high hopes that their child is going to become what they had wanted to become but could not.

What is required here is love and understanding. You think that the youngster has no hopes for his own life? He certainly has. Is he not disheartened? Yes, he most certainly is. Not only is he disheartened, he is heartbroken too. Hasn't he lost face in his circle of friends? Doesn't he feel guilty of wasting his parents' money? To all these questions, the answer is a plain 'yes'. But berating him is definitely not the answer. The answer is to understand his feelings. There is no need of pity. Empathy? Yes! Encouragement? Yes! The effort has to be made not only by parents, but also by the teachers and society to help this child, so that his self-confidence could be brought back. A message should go out to such children that failing or getting low marks once does not mean that he or she is a failure for life. All he needs to do is to put in more effort and if he cannot do it alone, then seek help. Or, if the subjects chosen by him for some reason are not to his liking, he should consider changing them.

We have dime-a-dozen instances where children turn down the parental profession and choose some other vocation. This hurts the parents no end. And, in the long run, it is seen that the children have excelled in the profession that they chose for themselves. Parental ego should be curbed, for ego has no role here or anywhere. A doctor's children do not have to be doctors. Just because the father has a nursing home, he would want his children to become doctors and run it later. I agree it is a very convenient scenario. But if the children have no propensity towards a career in medicine, they should not be forced into it. I feel that a satiated family is a happy family. A rich family might not be a happy one.

Parents should accept their children for what they are. The realisation that their children need not be the pillars of society, scholars, singers and sportsmen all rolled in one, is indispensable. For starters, they should be healthy. Parental love and understanding will keep them away from anti-social elements and drugs. The discipline and values that are imbibed in them will make them good citizens. The confidence that they boost in their children will make sure that they do not look for confidence boosting elsewhere. After all, we need good upright citizens primarily, who have value for their family systems. Being materialistic and rich is not what we need to insist upon.

I asked my secretary who, very much like most of us, is from the middle class. She has two sons who are now going to the college and I may add here, very polite and well-behaved. They are doing well in college. I asked her a hypothetical question. I said, "If your children had been bad at studies or duffers in common parlance, what would you have done?"

"Oh! I would have beaten them black and blue, like I have always been doing where studies were concerned. I had told their teacher that where studies were concerned, if she gave one slap to other non-achievers, she had my permission to give my children four!"

I said, "Beating does not change a poor student into a good student."

"Yes, but if they still did not study, I would have done what I had always warned them that I would do. I would have kicked them out of the house. They have a duty to themselves. They have to fend for themselves and then for the family which they would have. I have made it amply clear that I can't look after their needs for the rest of their lives. That much they know! It is because of the stick, and the knowledge that we will not cater to their needs indefinitely, that have made them slog and do well. Today we are creating a society of sissies who go running to their mothers for pocket money if they have to go on a date. Sissies, who have never been punished or who have never been on the receiving end of a stick or a slap! If the teacher scolds or slaps them, the whole town is up in arms. When we were in school, we were slapped and caned. Our parents never went and slapped the teacher. Discipline is needed all the more in today's world."

I agree to what she said. What about you?

I know of a family which is very unhappy. They have everything that anyone can hope for, except happiness. May be they have that too. They just don't know what part of the house it is lying in. The mother is authoritative and a perfectionist. She refuses to adjust with changing times. She has never been able to accept her children for what they are. Without realising she has been always comparing her three children with other children. It is natural that children will have some differences. Some would be taller, some would be smarter, and as they grow up, some might have done better financially. She tended to lose the qualities of her own children in the quagmire of collective qualities that she saw in the world. The expectations that she had from her children made her lose sight of the primary roles that each had in this world.

The sons objected to this trait of hers, but to no avail. She inadvertently played them against each other. Result? All sons, despite having done tolerably well for themselves, have very little confidence in themselves, and they have no love for each other.

She wanted hugely successful children for their own sake. Her parameter of success was always the bank balance and what they possessed. A house was of immense value. Her struggle in life was probably what lead her to think in those terms. I know of other parents who would go over board if their children achieved a small thing. Such children get such a huge boost in self esteem just by that one act by their parents.

I feel that people should be more demonstrative. If they love some one, they should tell them. They should hug each other more often. It wasn't that this lady in question did not love her children. There is no way that she didn't. But she totally lacked in the art of demonstrativeness. Remember. If you love your children, tell them. Show them. Do not leave it to the children to imagine the extent of the love that their parents have for them.

Grandparents

These are the grandmothers that we see mostly, though they are never the grandmothers in the true sense. They like their role of mother-in-law better and are in fact mother-in-law and grandmother rolled in one.

It has been said that the perfect grandmother is a paragon of virtue. She is loving and helpful, never interferes and never offers an opinion unless asked for. This is a fantasy grandmother, but then one can at least try.

When children arrive, grandparents are not far behind in this state of ecstasy. They are genuinely fond of their grandchildren.

If I had known grandchildren were so much fun, I would have had them before my children.

...a grandparent

These are the days when the intelligent and highly educated daughter-in-law decides to live separately from her interfering in-laws. Out goes the support system of the oldies! They do not mind missing out on the support system, because of the domestic help that is easily available in India. Children can be conveniently sent to crèches where they are looked after fairly well. But if she is living abroad with her husband, she is the sweetest daughter-in-law anyone can have this side or the other side of Suez Canal. She is ready to send her tickets with entreaties of 'come visit us in the States, mom'. This happens only when she has delivered her child. Foreign shores provide everything except cheap nannies. So, the cheapest ones available are from good old India in the garb of Mom (hers or his). Hardly matters!

These emotional women, the Moms, will no doubt lug their husbands along, but that is a hazard the 'children' happily endure. The elders will cook, clean and look after their grandchild. They will even take their child out for a stroll in the garden.

The latest technique adopted by a daughter was unique. This lady calls up her mother and tells her to come to the States to visit them. She sends her a one way ticket. The mother reaches her daughter, does what she is supposed to for the family for a few months. One day, the daughter takes her for sightseeing in a park so remote that even a thorough-bred American would find it difficult not to get lost. She tells her mamma, "Mamma, please sit here while I get something to munch on."

Now, the illiterate mamma did not that her darling daughter was not coming back. The lost mamma is picked up by a patrol officer, who does not know the language she speaks. He takes her to the police station. Once they ascertain her nationality, they take her to the Indian Embassy. Since the daughter has her mamma's passport, so mamma does not know where she lives or where her daughter lives. Ultimately, she is deported back to India. Lovely daughter has succeeded in saving the return fare too!

Parents of these children who are settled abroad have understood the game, but they can do nothing about it. They are in love with their children and grandchildren. The tight emotional noose gets tighter with the passing years. Problem is that they have no friends in an alien country. If there are more of their kind, they are suffering from the same paradox. Ultimately, they beseech their children to let them go back home.

It is not that these children do not love their parents. They do, but then they are so caught up in their own problems and their daily rituals that bringing up children becomes very difficult. They look towards the shores that they have left behind and see their parents, four of them living there with apparently nothing to do. So they send them invitations to visit them. The babysitting is a camouflaged, built in carrot which no grandparent can miss out on. And they come running! The rest is history.

PART 4

Empty Nest Syndrome

As our journey nears its end, we find that we are old. Our children have grown. They have to find their own destinies and they cannot do that sitting in the comfort zones of their parents' house. They have to go out into the open world and look out for greener pastures. Our children are forced to leave their nests, so to say. Most of them are happy doing so. But that leaves the old parents in a situation called the 'Empty Nest Syndrome'. This situation is certainly not an easy one for parents. All of a sudden, they are alone. They have only each other. The circle is once again complete. They are back to the time when they were living with their parents in an extended family. Once children came into their world, their existence revolved around the children. Living alone as husband and wife seems almost a forgotten dream.

They are out of practice. They have even forgotten how to interact with each other without a third party.

It is almost like the father's retirement. He is at sea with nothing to do.

Earlier, he had a routine. He got up in the morning, dressed up to go to the office, did his work and came back home to his family in the evening. All of a sudden, after getting up in the morning he does not know where to start the day from.

Similarly, when the children depart, parents have to learn, all over again, the art of staying together as a couple, sharing life together, of the basics of give and take, the subtle art of staying out of each others' hair and way, so that they do not trip over the other person. In other words, they have to fall in love with each other, all over again. Most important of all, they have to learn how to stay without their children. It is a tough ask, a tough learning experience at an age when they have forgotten most of the things that people still have to learn.

Every parent does not succeed. The wife has already mastered the art of nagging. The husband, when he was young, was in a position to retaliate. But now, he no longer has the energy to confront her. He looks for ways and means to stay out of the house. The golf bug bites again. Many of them become deft bridge players. Hence someone said:

My wife has made me join the bridge club.
I jump next Tuesday.

Some husbands begin to interfere in the matters of the house. This bugs the wife to no end. So, she joins the ladies for Mahjong and forms a card club. In a way, they have separate lives. It works well for them.

Meanwhile, they wait for their children to come home!

Conclusion

I am surprised at myself. This book did not turn out the way I intended it to. I had thought out a different ending. I had envisaged this book to be a humorous one, all the while trying to poke fun at the institution of marriage. During the last six months or so, since I have been on it, I have been talking to a host of people who have gladly given me their opinion on the subject of marriage and children. I am indebted to them.

You could ask me the reason for choosing to write on a subject which has been debated and written about till it is thread bare. But whatever has been debated and written is in the Western context.

After the huge success of my previous book, *Please Mom! It's My Life*, which was basically a book to educate the masses, especially the younger lot, to understand life… at the right time, I thought it appropriate to write *MARRIAGE ROCKS!* as a sequel. The rising number of divorces in the early phases, the high percentage of drug abuse in children and the parent-children feuds, sibling rivalry because of increasing materialism, made me choose this subject. The response to the book justified the subject. It was as if a lot of people would love to be a part of it.

As I wrote, met people and wrote some more, I was forced to introspect and re-examine my own married life of 33 years. I relived the good and the bad times and found that the good far outweighed the tough times. Getting married was indeed the best thing that could have happened to me and indeed, to everyone whom I interviewed. The joy that we have received through our children and now through our grandchildren is simply incomparable. I cannot imagine anything else that could have made us happier.

Indians are very different. We are a breed apart! We are one of the oldest civilisations of the world. Marriage in our country is an accepted part of our existence. One need not debate on it. Only in India is the husband called *'Pati Parameshwar'*. Remember the story of Savitri and Satyavan, where she snatched her husband's life back from Yamraj, after he had died. This story only tells us that if the wife is as strong, determined and loving as Savitri, she can even bring back her husband from death. That is our cultural heritage. That was the basis of *sati*, where the wife prefers death to separation from her husband. The Indian woman will reign supreme in the world if only our cultural heritage is revisited.

I am not saying that I am for *sati*. I am totally against it. I am against divorce, or if I may say that I am against the ease with which it is available in the present times. In the south of India, certain customs still prevail where the wedding ceremonies go on for 7-8 days, through the day and night, only to make the bride and bridegroom realise how tough getting married is, and for them to remember how they went through the rigours of the marriage ceremony. If at all the thought of divorce arises, the memory of the wedding ceremony will make them reconsider their decision. I agree that there are circumstances where living together is hell for the two of them and the best course is separation. The word used is 'irreconcilable' differences, but if this term is used too frequently and too easily, that shows that there is no effort on the part of the couple to reconcile.

We have customs in India, where the couple after having been married for 20-40 years, goes through the wedding ceremony again! This why would need a full chapter.

It is only in recent times that we have been inundated with Western influence, through movies and the print media, the corporate culture and the sexual revolution, if you would care to call it that. Our youngsters are overawed. Quite a few of them have been, quite frankly bowled over.

The joys that we shared as a couple and then as a family, the happiness that we felt at every milestone of our children, the events that were hallmarks in our journey to where we have reached and the journey we still are on, the sharing of so many things but most of all the love that we have for each other, are some things that I would never have felt if I had not been married. We would have been islands in the vast blue sea of life, each one of us living in our own little cocoon.

When our children get married into families which are God sent, the union makes us ever so strong. It is such a unique phenomenon, that two families in their own selfish interests, get bonded together to give each other so much solace. It is possible that I might have used an inappropriate word 'selfish' here. But each one, to begin with, has the best interest of his own child. Everyone wants his son or daughter to get the best partner so that he or she is happy for the rest of his or her life. As a fallout, the best interest of the person who is coming into their family is seen. I am not talking about the crooks. This world is full of good people. It is the handful of crooked people who mar the beauty of our world. Even the most dreaded mother-in-law is not as bad as she is made out to be. There are mothers-in-law like the one my daughter-in-law has. She has already developed a halo behind her head. I know of so many ladies who are such wonderful mothers-in-law. I also am aware of a host of young brides who will make ideal partners for their husbands and assets to the family that they have entered.

I see my friends around me. Most of them have satisfied married lives. Of course each of them has had his marital hurricanes, cyclones and twisters. But they have survived! The happiest of them all are the grandparents. The happiness that their own children gave them at each stage of their lives… when they were born, started their milestones, went up their academic ladders, jumped on their professional escalators and then finally settling down in their marital lives, is incomparable. All these stages were interrupted by sickness. There could have been failures, because in life there can never be just successes. If there had been no failures, success would not have been so sweet. Grandchildren are the greatest gifts that our children can give to us as parents. Grandparents are there to enjoy their grandchildren, because they are never directly involved in their education, tantrums and sicknesses. That aspect belongs exclusively to their parents. Grandparents have already done their bit amply, while bringing up their own children, haven't they?

I looked at people who had made it big in the world of marriage. It was total teamwork, with the husband in the role of captain, steering their ship through the high and low tides. There were sacrifices galore. At the end of the tunnel, they always saw light!

But this world is real. There are people who have burnt their daughters-in-law for their greed. We talk about 'middle class morality' when it is convenient to us. Middle class morality is no longer an accepted point worth arguing. The middle class, the protagonists would say, is the persecuted one as far as morality goes. The rich can drink, smoke, do substance abuse and take infidelity to great heights. No one minds. These are the norms of the upper class. Similarly the lower classes, they say, have no morals. They do exactly the same things the upper class does. No one can point a finger at them because they will point a foot at you. But if the middle class dabbles in any of these, they are immediately hauled up by society. Let me remind the protagonists of the so-called middle class morality, that all cases of bride burning take place solely in the middle class. I would say that whatever the upper class and the lower class might be guilty of, they never burn their brides. If the middle class stops burning their brides and switches to smoking, consuming drugs and dabbling with each other sexually, I promise to look the other way. (They are already into these things in a big way though!)

There is no crime in the world that is worse than torching a living human being. What is the bride's crime? Bringing in less dowry! Is this a crime? There are some who have premeditated the act, even before the wedding takes place. Are we human beings? No matter what, burning a fellow human being can never be justified. On 23rd of June 2007, we had the latest bride-burning incident in our ignominious tradition. While in Nigeria in 1982, I was shown news items about bride burning almost every day. I would hang my head in shame. They would tell me, "If you don't want the ruddy woman, just kick her out of the house, divorce her, but for God's sake, why burn the poor little thing?"

There have been men and women who have killed their spouses because of their extra-marital affairs. There have been mothers who have committed suicide, killing their own children; and there have been fathers who have killed their entire families. But then all kinds of people make up this world. We cannot and should not denounce the institution of marriage just because a few people were on the receiving end of rough treatment. Too bad for them! On the other hand, there are thousands and thousands of married couples who are happily rearing their families.

All children do not turn out badly. There are more children who turn out good than bad. These good ones study well, are respectful to their elders, do not get into drugs, get good jobs, do well in businesses in India and abroad, marry happily and settle down. Yes! I would just hope that the sibling rivalry due to the materialism of this world ends.

I would end here with the hope that if I am reborn in this world and I find the institution of marriage as preserved as it is today, I get to marry the same lady that I am married to and have the same children that I have. That is, if they would want me too!

But Nikhaar Budhiraja begs to differ.

She would like to be the parent to her present parents in her next birth!

∞

The End

or

Is it the Beginning...?

By the Same Author

Please, Mom! It's My Life

A book for teenagers and young adults who think they know everything

For some inexplicable reason, puberty and adolescence produce a streak in children, which automatically closes their eyes and ears to what their parents want them to see and hear. However, these two organs open wide when their friends say something. It is really funny.

Hence, these adolescents carry on doing what they want to do and not what their parents would want them to do. Of course, there are exceptions to the rule. It is wrong for the children to be blamed all the time. Sometimes, parents are just not there for them.

Since I am totally against the 'blame game', I had to find out ways and means to help children and people till the age of 35, for I feel that after that, no matter what you tell them, it rarely helps. I realised that by lecturing on the subject of stress busting and how to live life, the message will be reaching only a few.

Hence the book *Please, Mom! It's My Life* is authored by Dr. Jaideep Singh Chadha exclusively for the adolescents and their way of life.

Pages: 152
Price: Rs. 120/- • Postage: Rs. 15/-
